Caught On The Hop

A Comedy

Derek Benfield

A Samuel French Acting Edition

SAMUELFRENCH-LONDON.CO.UK
SAMUELFRENCH.COM

Copyright © 1979 by Derek Benfield
Copyright © 2000 Revised by Derek Benfield
All Rights Reserved

CAUGHT ON THE HOP is fully protected under the copyright laws of the British Commonwealth, including Canada, the United States of America, and all other countries of the Copyright Union. All rights, including professional and amateur stage productions, recitation, lecturing, public reading, motion picture, radio broadcasting, television and the rights of translation into foreign languages are strictly reserved.

ISBN 978-0-573-11066-5

www.samuelfrench-london.co.uk

www.samuelfrench.com

For Amateur Production Enquiries

United Kingdom and World excluding North America

plays@SamuelFrench-London.co.uk

020 7255 4302/01

Each title is subject to availability from Samuel French,

depending upon country of performance.

CAUTION: Professional and amateur producers are hereby warned that *CAUGHT ON THE HOP* is subject to a licensing fee. Publication of this play does not imply availability for performance. Both amateurs and professionals considering a production are strongly advised to apply to the appropriate agent before starting rehearsals, advertising, or booking a theatre. A licensing fee must be paid whether the title is presented for charity or gain and whether or not admission is charged.

The professional rights in this play are controlled by The Agency Ltd, 24 Pottery Lane, Holland Park, London W11 4LZ.

No one shall make any changes in this title for the purpose of production. No part of this book may be reproduced, stored in a retrieval system, or transmitted in any form, by any means, now known or yet to be invented, including mechanical, electronic, photocopying, recording, videotaping, or otherwise, without the prior written permission of the publisher. No one shall upload this title, or part of this title, to any social media websites.

The right of Derek Benfield to be identified as author of this work has been asserted by him in accordance with Section 77 of the Copyright, Designs and Patents Act 1988

CAUGHT ON THE HOP

First presented by Mark Furness on a national tour which opened at the Gateway Theatre, Chester, on 1st February 1977, with the following cast in order of appearance:

George	Derek Benfield
Phil	Richard Easton
Mrs Puffet	Sheila Collings
Julie	Primi Townsend
Maggie	Margaret Ashcroft
Mr Brasset	Trevor Griffiths
Greta	Sally Harrison
Alan	Clifford Earl

Directed by **Jan Butlin**
Setting by **Pamela Ingram**

This revised version of the play was first presented by Sally Hughes at The Mill at Sonning Dinner Theatre on 14th January 1997, with the following cast:

George	Timothy Carlton
Phil	Martyn Stanbridge
Mrs Puffet	Margaret Ashcroft
Julie	Suzy Aitchison
Maggie	Carolyn Lyster
Mr Brasset	Barrie Gosney
Greta	Rebecca Lloyd
Alan	Will Ashcroft

Directed by **Dennis Ramsden**
Setting by **Peter D Szak**

CHARACTERS

George, a good friend
Phil, an incurable romantic
Mrs Puffet, an observant cleaning lady
Julie, a romantic young girl
Maggie, a tolerant wife
Mr Brasset, a puzzled fireman
Greta, an angry young lady
Alan, a bewildered lover

The action takes place in Phil's and Maggie's house in a pleasant suburb

ACT I

    Scene 1   A summer afternoon

    Scene 2   The same evening

ACT II   A few seconds later

Time: the present

Other plays by Derek Benfield published by Samuel French Ltd

Anyone for Breakfast?
Bedside Manners
Beyond a Joke
A Bird in the Hand
Don't Lose the Place!
Fish Out of Water
A Fly in the Ointment
Flying Feathers
In for the Kill
Look Who's Talking
Off the Hook
Panic Stations
Post Horn Gallop
Running Riot
A Toe in the Water
Touch and Go
Two and Two Together
Up and Running
Wild Goose Chase

ACT I

Scene 1

The living-room of Maggie and Phil's house in a leafy suburb. It is a warm, sunny afternoon

The room is bright and attractive. Large windows open out on to a patio leading to the pleasant garden and on the opposite side double doors lead to the hall and main entrance. There is also a door to the kitchen and a bow window through which you can look out into the street

About the walls are a number of paintings of varying styles that have been executed by Maggie with varying degrees of success

George is coming in quickly from the hall, looking for Phil

George Phil! Phil!

George goes out into the garden to look

(*Off*) Phil! Phil!

Phil comes in quickly from the kitchen, looking for George

Phil George! George!

Phil goes into the hall to look

(*Off*) George! George!

George returns from the garden

George Phil! Phil!

George goes into the kitchen to look

(*Off*) Phil! Phil!

Phil returns from the hall

Phil George! George!

George returns from the kitchen

George Phil! Phil! (*He sees Phil*) Ah! There you are!
Phil (*smiling, delightedly*) I heard you arrive.
George I'm not surprised. I drove into the back of a car out there!
Phil You didn't!
George Little three-wheeler. Not *yours*, I hope?
Phil No, not *mine*...
George That's all right, then.
Phil You shouldn't have been driving so fast.
George Well, you said it was important. (*He goes to Phil, urgently*) Right! What's it all about?

Phil gives a big, dreamy smile. George looks alarmed

Oh, no! You haven't done it again? *Please* say you haven't done it again.
Phil I've done it again.
George Oh, my God...!
Phil I knew you'd be pleased.
George I'm *not* pleased! Phil—why do you *do* it?
Phil (*romantically*) I can't resist them. They look so helpless and appealing. It brings out the best in me.
George The *beast*, more likely!
Phil No, no! I want to look after them and protect them...

George sighs, long-sufferingly

George All right—how old's *this* one?
Phil (*shrugging vaguely*) Twenty-three, twenty-four...
George You said you were going in for more mature women.
Phil That was before I met Julie...
George Is *that* her name?
Phil What's wrong with it?
George Nothing's wrong with it. Makes a change from Yasmin.
Phil What?
George The last one! I expected her to come in wearing a yashmak!
Phil (*defensively*) Well, she didn't!
George No. Hardly wore anything at all.
Phil This one's different...

Act I, Scene 1

George Oh—fully clothed. Well, that's something. Doesn't she mind that you're already married?

Phil (*vaguely*) H'm?

George You haven't told her!

Phil It didn't seem to fit into the conversation.

George Goodbye, Phil! (*He starts to go*)

Phil (*following him*) You can't walk out on me!

George Yes, I can!

Phil (*restraining him*) But, George—you're my oldest friend. I need your help.

George Look—I did your dirty work last time. I broke the news to Yasmin about you being married, and what happened? She forgave *you* and hit *me*!

Phil Well, you were my best man.

George I didn't think it would be a full-time job! What did Maggie say?

Phil (*vaguely*) H'm?

George Your wife! What did *she* say?

Phil Well, I...

George (*appalled*) You haven't told her, have you?

Phil smiles, innocently

Phil You're so good at it, George.

George I should be. I've had enough practise. Maggie has only to come in and see me looking furtive and she knows what's coming.

Phil Thanks, George! I knew I could rely on you. (*He shakes his hand, vigorously*)

George (*extricating himself*) I didn't say I'd do it!

Phil I'll get you a drink. (*He hastens away to pour a large whisky*)

George (*following him*) In the middle of the afternoon?

Phil Well, it is a celebration.

George Maggie's far too good for you. Far too tolerant. Thanks. (*He accepts the whisky*) How long's *this* one going to last?

Phil Knowing you, not very long.

George Not the whisky—the girl!

Phil (*dreamily*) Oh—for *ever*. This is the real thing...

George Nonsense. It'll be passing traffic, same as all the others. Maggie'll simply paint a couple of pictures and wait till it's over like she always has before. (*He sips his whisky, gratefully*)

Phil (*heavily*) No, George. This one's serious. I shall have to divorce Maggie...

George chokes on his drink

George Why on earth should you divorce Maggie?

Phil Because I told Julie that I'd marry *her*.

George You *should* have told her you'd got a wife already!

Phil Oh, George—I couldn't do that. Not when she'd just asked me to marry her.

George stares at him in total disbelief

George Julie asked you to marry her?

Phil Well, I may not be *your* type, but I do appeal to *some* people!

George You should have said no!

Phil I hadn't got the heart. You know how romantic I am. (*Romantically*) There we were on top of the 49 bus...

George (*wearily*) Oh, no—not the 49 bus *again*...!

Phil Ducks on the pond, the sun shining, the birds singing. I just couldn't refuse her.

George Well, you should have done!

Phil I didn't want to upset her. You know me, George. I can't bear seeing women cry...

George Then you'll just have to close your eyes and tell her you've changed your mind!

Phil I can't do that.

George Why not?

Phil I'm moving in with her tomorrow.

George What?!

Phil There didn't seem any point in hanging about.

George You certainly didn't do that! Moving in where?

Phil Ah—yes—well, Julie has this friend, you see. And Julie's friend is married. (*Impressively*) And she and her husband—have a *house*.

George So?

Phil Well, they've decided to go abroad for a while and they're lending their house to Julie!

George And you're moving in with her?

Phil Yes.

George Tomorrow?

Phil Yes.

George I see...

Phil There is one slight snag.

George I thought there might be.

Phil It's a bit near home.

George How near?

Phil Next door.

George (*appalled*) You can't move in next door!

Phil Why not?

Act I, Scene 1

George What about Maggie?
Phil She'll still be living *here*.
George Exactly! Next door to *you*!
Phil (*ingenuously*) Actually, it might work out rather well. She'll know where to find me, won't she?
George You think she'll *want* to find you?
Phil (*trying to be patient*) George... she's not going to stop loving me simply because I'm married to someone else.
George You reckon?
Phil And I still love *her*. (*Romantically*) I shall go on looking after her like I have before. A fuse blows and I'll be up the ladder! The gas goes wonky and I'll be there to fix it!
George You think she'll *want* you popping in and out all the time?
Phil Of course she will. You forget, George—I'm very handy in the house.
George Well, now you're going to be handy in *two* houses!

Phil activates himself and goes to look at the sofa

Phil Now, then—what about *this*?
George (*disinterestedly*) What about what?
Phil The sofa! Do you think she'll miss it?
George Why should she miss it?
Phil Good! That's what *I* thought!
George (*puzzled*) Phil... if Maggie's still living here, why should she miss the sofa?
Phil Ah. Yes. Well... (*He smiles, a little embarrassed*)

George gazes at him, appalled

George You're not going to take it *with* you?
Phil (*reasonably*) Well, Julie's providing the house. The least *I* can do is to take some bits of furniture.

George is speechless

Mrs Puffet, the daily help, comes sailing in from the hall

Puffet I'm usually away by now.
Phil Well, why aren't you?

Mrs Puffet gives George a hard look

Puffet Perhaps *he* knows.

Phil Do you, George?
George Knows what?
Puffet Was you, wasn't it?
George What was?
Puffet The one who put a stop to my departure!
Phil (*shocked*) George!
George What are you talking about?
Puffet My little banger! Parked outside!
George (*to Phil*) *Her* little banger?
Phil (*enjoying George's discomfort*) Yes. Motor banger. Three-wheeler. She uses it for coming and going.

George glares at him

Puffet Only this time there'll be no going. Not till I get it mended.
George W-what's that got to do with me?
Puffet (*glaring at him*) *Someone* put a dint in my behind. I'll have to be towed away. There'll be no starting me now.
Phil (*quietly*) No stopping you, either, by the sound of it.
Puffet I see they're moving.
Phil Who?
Puffet Them next door.
Phil Moving?
Puffet Out.
Phil What?
George Them next door.
Phil Oh. Yes. That's right. They are. They have.
Puffet There'll be new ones, I suspect?
Phil Moving in?
Puffet That's what I suspect.
Phil Yes. That's right. There are.
Puffet How many?
Phil Er ... two. One of each kind.
Puffet Well, that's something, I suppose. These days you never know. *Young* couple, are they?
Phil (*modestly*) Er—yes. Yes, you could say that.
George Could you? (*He laughs*)

Phil glares at him

Puffet I hope they're not like the last lot.
George Oh? What were *they* like?
Puffet (*heavily*) Free parties.

Act I, Scene 1

George You mean you didn't have to pay?
Puffet Morally free!
Phil Good heavens! And I never knew.
Puffet You can never tell *what's* going on behind closed curtains.
Phil I must remember that...
Puffet Sexually abandoned, they was!
Phil (*shocked*) In the suburbs?
Puffet That's where it thrives. (*To George, indicating Phil*) That's what I like about him and his wife. They're not sexually abandoned.

The men exchange a look. Mrs Puffet turns to Phil

So let's hope these new people are nice.
Phil Oh, yes, they are! I mean—I'm sure they *will* be. Very nice.
Puffet In that case I might be able to give them a couple of my p.ms.
George P.ms?
Puffet Afternoons.
George Yes, of course. (*To Phil*) Do you think they'd like a couple of her p.ms?
Phil (*alarmed*) Ah—well—er——
Puffet All my a.ms is spoken for!
George Yes, I bet they are...
Puffet But I do have a few p.ms going begging.
Phil I'll have a word with them, Mrs Puffet. But they're probably fixed up already.
Puffet Be nice and handy if I do the two. I can pop backwards and forwards, can't I?
George You won't be the only one...!

Phil glares at him

Puffet Leave you to it, then. I'll finish off elsewhere.

Mrs Puffet goes out into the hall

George looks severely at Phil

George It was *her* little banger!
Phil Yes. Didn't I tell you?
George No, you didn't! (*He goes to look out of the window, anxiously*)
Phil You don't have to worry. It only had three wheels to start with.

At that moment Julie arrives from the hall. Pretty, yes. Appealing, yes. And laden with luggage. A suitcase, carrier bags, parcels and things. She sees Phil, drops her luggage and runs to him, delightedly. She does not see George

Julie Darling!
Phil (*alarmed*) You're early! We said tomorrow. I'm not ready!

Julie finishes up in his arms. Phil laughs nervously, a bit embarrassed with George watching from behind Julie. He extricates himself

No, Julie...!
Julie What?
Phil Not *here*.
Julie But I love you! (*She embraces him again*)
Phil Yes. I don't mean that. I mean not *this* one.
Julie Sorry?
Phil (*extricating himself again*) The other one! The one next door!
Julie What are you talking about?
Phil The house next door. Your friend's house is next door. *This* is number four.
Julie Oh, no—how awful! I saw your car outside this one and the front door was open so I came straight in.
Phil Blast Mrs Puffet!
Julie What?
Phil She's always opening things and leaving them.
Julie Who's Mrs Puffet?
Phil Ah.
Julie Well?
Phil Yes.
Julie Are you feeling all right?
Phil Never better!
Julie Then what are you doing in a strange house?
Phil Am I?
Julie That's what you said. Not this one, the other one. So what are you doing in this one?
George (*behind Julie*) Perhaps *I* can help?

Julie jumps a mile

Julie Ooh!
George Sorry. I made you jump.
Phil Yes, you did. She went right up in the air.
Julie I didn't see you there.

Act I, Scene 1 9

Phil This is George. George, this is Julie.
George How do you do.

George and Julie shake hands

Phil George is an old friend of mine.
George Getting older every minute...
Julie Oh, I see! So that's why you were here. This is *George's* house!
Phil Yes!
George (*appalled*) What?!
Phil That's right. This is George's house!

George glares at him

Julie Well, isn't that lucky?
Phil Is it?
Julie Yes. Now we'll be living next door to your old friend George.
Phil So we will! How nice! (*He beams at George*)

George looks far from pleased. Julie links arms with them both, affectionately

Julie I can see we three are going to get on like a house on fire. Have you known him very long?
George (*dismally*) Yes. Years and years and years...
Julie I only met him last week but already I feel I know all there is to know about him.
George I wouldn't be too sure about that!
Julie You mean he's got hidden depths?
George He's got depths all right. Let's hope they *remain* hidden.
Phil What?
George (*pointedly*) Well, the front door may still be open—and *my wife* will be back at any minute.
Phil Oh, God!
Julie Oh, good! I'd like to meet her.
Phil No, you wouldn't! Come on, darling! (*He starts to collect up her luggage and pile it on to her*) Have you got the key?
Julie Key?
Phil To the house.
Julie Why should I have the key to George's house?
Phil Not this one. The one next door.
Julie Oh, yes. I've got that. But aren't *you* coming?
Phil No. Not yet. You go ahead. Let yourself in and have a look around.
Julie Why can't you come with me?

Phil I've got things to see to.
Julie *Here?*
Phil Yes.
Julie What things?
Phil Loose ends.
George Very loose.
Julie In *this* house?
George (*quickly*) *My* loose ends! He was helping me tidy them up.
Phil I shan't be a second.
Julie All right, then. But hurry. (*She starts to go towards the hall*)
Phil No! (*He grabs her and pulls her back*)
Julie What?
Phil This way! (*He urges her towards the garden*)
Julie (*puzzled*) Does it make any difference?
Phil Someone might see you coming out.
Julie Would that matter?
Phil Might give them the wrong idea. Make them think things about George.
Julie Oh, I see. Well, we mustn't do that, must we? Mustn't let them think things about George. Goodbye, George!
George Goodbye.

Julie turns to Phil and they kiss quickly in between goodbyes

Julie Goodbye, darling!
Phil Goodbye!
Julie Goodbye!
Phil Goodbye!
Julie Goodbye!
Phil Goodbye!
Julie Goodbye!

Julie runs out into the garden

George Is she going for *ever*?
Phil When you're young you're romantic, George.
George I must remember that...

Phil goes to George, urgently

Phil Well? What do you think of her?
George (*brusquely*) Never mind all that!
Phil What's wrong with her?
George Nothing's wrong with her.

Act I, Scene 1   11

Phil You don't like her. I can tell.
George Yes, I do. She's very nice. Very pretty. Very young. I like her.
Phil Good.
George Now can we talk about *us*? (*He grabs Phil's arm and pulls him close*)
Phil Oh, George, I didn't know you cared.
George (*hastily releasing Phil's arm*) You know what I mean!
Phil You do sound fierce.
George I *am* fierce. All of a sudden I've got a house I didn't even want!
Phil Well, what else could I have said?
George You could have denied it.
Phil Would have been so abrupt. You've got to ease into these things, George.
George You should have told her you were married there and then.
Phil I didn't get the chance! Anyhow, I couldn't tell *her* before I told Maggie.
George Well, you should have told Maggie before Julie moved in!
Phil That wasn't my fault. She wasn't supposed to move in until tomorrow. So *you*'ll have to explain to Maggie.
George That you want a divorce? No fear!
Phil But you're so good at that sort of thing. So diplomatic. Right! That's settled. Come and give me a hand with this.

They go to either end of the sofa

George You're not *really* taking it with you?
Phil Of course I am!
George Won't Julie think it a bit odd if we start trundling through *her* front door with *my* sofa?
Phil I'll say you lent it to us. Come on! Through the garden and round the back.

Reluctantly, George helps Phil lift the sofa. They prepare to move towards the garden

Maggie sails in from the hall. She is a well-dressed, attractive woman with a dry sense of humour. She is carrying some shopping and various items of painting equipment. She is talking as she comes in

Maggie Sorry I'm late, darling. I hope you got yourself some tea. (*She stops, seeing them*)

They freeze, the sofa still off the ground

What on earth are you doing?

Phil We didn't hear you arriving.
Maggie Next time I'll ring a fire bell. (*Puzzled, she puts some of her things down and then looks at them again*) Why don't you put it down?
Phil Ah. Yes. It is a bit heavy.

Phil puts his end of the sofa down and goes to Maggie, leaving George with his end still off the ground

Hullo, darling. Good class?
Maggie Yes, thank you. (*Loudly*) George!

George drops the sofa on his foot and cries out in pain

George Ooh!
Maggie You're looking very furtive.
George A-a-am I?
Maggie (*suspiciously*) You haven't got anything to *tell* me, have you?
George No!

Phil glares at him

Phil (*whispering*) Yes, you have!
George (*whispering*) No, I haven't!
Maggie What were you doing with the sofa?

Phil is blank for a moment, then turns to George

Phil What were we doing with the sofa, George?
George (*helpfully*) Taking it into the garden?
Phil (*to Maggie*) Taking it into the garden.
Maggie Why on earth should you want to take the sofa into the garden?

Phil is blank for a moment, then turns to George again

Phil George?
George It ... it's such a lovely day.
Phil Yes! (*To Maggie*) So we thought we'd take it out and sun on it in the sit. Er—sit on it in the sun!
Maggie What about the garden chairs?
Phil They're in the shed.
Maggie Then get them *out* of the shed.
Phil Oh, they're so boring, garden chairs. I never did like them. All that business of opening them up and adjusting them. I always get my fingers caught.

Act I, Scene 1

Maggie So you thought it would be easier to take the sofa into the garden?
Phil Yes—exactly!

Maggie gives him a weary look and sorts out her painting things. Phil hovers, nervously

Paint anything exciting today, darling? Bowl of fruit? Something like that? (*He picks up a frame containing two canvases*)
Maggie You know very well I'm not still on still life.
Phil (*with a grin*) It wasn't that pretty girl with her clothes off again, was it? (*He peers hopefully at the canvases*)
Maggie Why do you pretend to be interested? You know it bores you silly.
Phil Nothing of the sort. Got them all over the walls, haven't we? (*To George*) She did all these, you know.
George Really? (*He looks at one with great enthusiasm*) Very nice!
Phil Not that one, you fool! That's a calendar from the Express Dairy.
Maggie Mrs Puffet tells me there are some new people moving in next door.
Phil Ah. She told you that, did she?
Maggie A *young* couple, she said. That's nice, isn't it?
Phil Is it?
Maggie I never did like the last lot. Awfully dull pair they were.
George Not when they had the curtains drawn.
Maggie Let's hope this lot are more friendly. We'd better invite them in.
Phil No!!
Maggie (*surprised by his vehemence*) Why not?
Phil Well, they—they've hardly had time to unpack. Have they, George?
George No. And they haven't moved the furniture in, either! (*He grins at Phil and plods off to the drinks table*)
Maggie All the same, it wouldn't be very neighbourly to ignore them, would it? I'll ask them in for drinks.
Phil We haven't enough!
Maggie Don't say George has finished the whisky already?
George (*caught in the act*) Not yet...! (*He pours a quick one and downs it in one*)
Maggie I wonder what they're like...
George (*enthusiastically*) Oh, *she's very* pretty.
Maggie What about him?
George *Not* so pretty... (*He laughs*)
Phil (*glaring at George*) We haven't met him yet!
George Haven't we?
Phil Of course we haven't!
George Ah—of course we haven't! I forgot...
Phil (*to Maggie*) Apparently he's very secretive. Doesn't come out very often. Bit of a recluse.

Maggie Oh, dear... What does he do?
George (*amused*) A lot of running!
Phil George...!
Maggie Running?
George Yes. Backwards and forwards—across the common!
Maggie You mean he's athletic?
George Oh, yes. Likes to keep in trim. Always dashing about in a blue track suit.
Maggie (*to Phil*) I thought you said he didn't come out very often.
Phil No—he doesn't! (*He glares at George*)
George But when he does he's always running.

Mrs Puffet comes in with her hat and coat on

Puffet The garage on the corner says they can beat me out and re-spray me by the morning, so I could do with a pair of strong men.
Phil (*quietly*) Yes, I bet she could...!
Puffet I'll be back directly, madam. Then I shall do those things that I have left undone.

Mrs Puffet goes out into the hall

Phil I should think she's done enough already.
Maggie What was she talking about?
Phil Some dreadful driver drove into the back of her banger. (*He grins at George*) Come on, George! We'll give her a push.

Phil and George disappear into the hall

Maggie shrugs, puzzled, and continues sorting her paintings

Julie runs in from the garden, enthusiastically

Julie Darling! Do hurry up! I'm... (*She sees Maggie and stops*) Oh. Sorry.

Maggie is naturally rather surprised by a strange girl bursting into her house

Maggie Can I help you?
Julie I don't know. Do you live here?
Maggie This *is* number four, isn't it?
Julie Yes.
Maggie Then I live here.
Julie Ah! So you must be his wife? (*Meaning George's wife*)

Act I, Scene 1   15

Maggie Yes. I am. (*Meaning Phil's*) Forgive me if I just put these down, won't you? (*She puts down the paintings*)
Julie Oo—are you an artist?
Maggie (*modestly*) Well, I dabble a little.
Julie I wish I could paint. It must be so exciting!
Maggie Well, today our model was a rather fat man with goose pimples. I did *just* manage to control myself.
Julie (*studying the paintings on the walls*) Are these all yours?
Maggie Most of them, yes.
Julie Super...

Maggie has no idea who Julie is

Maggie Were you ... looking for someone?
Julie Yes. I thought he might still be here.
Maggie Who?
Julie My boyfriend.
Maggie (*puzzled*) Here?
Julie Yes. He came in to talk to an old friend of his who lives here. (*She makes the obvious deduction*) Ah! That means that my boyfriend...
Maggie Is an old friend of my husband's!
Julie Yes! You didn't see him, then?
Maggie I'm afraid not. Never mind. My husband will be back in a minute, then we can ask him where he's hidden your boyfriend. I... I don't remember seeing you before. Do you live near here?
Julie We didn't. But we do now.
Maggie Oh. Whereabouts?
Julie Next door.
Maggie Ah! I see! You're the young couple who are just moving in?
Julie Yes.
Maggie Well—congratulations!
Julie Oh, we're not married. Not yet.
Maggie Very few people are these days. Look—as you've only just moved in, you won't want to bother about cooking tonight—so why don't you and your boyfriend come to dinner with me and my husband?
Julie Oh. Well, thank you. That would be lovely.
Maggie But I hope he won't be too energetic!
Julie (*puzzled*) Energetic over dinner?
Maggie I don't want him getting my husband into a track suit and chasing him all over the common! (*She laughs*)
Julie (*bewildered*) Why on earth should he do that?
Maggie Well, you know what these athletic types are like.
Julie (*puzzled*) He never said anything to *me* about being athletic.

Maggie Didn't he?
Julie No.
Maggie How long have you known him?
Julie (*shyly*) Only a week...
Maggie Oh. Well, I expect he's going to surprise you. Spring it on you when you least expect it! (*She chuckles*)
Julie (*apprehensively*) Oh, dear...
Maggie Is that fixed, then, er... Sorry, I don't know your name.
Julie Julie.
Maggie That's fixed, then, Julie?
Julie What?
Maggie Dinner tonight.
Julie Oh. Yes. Thanks.
Maggie About half seven?
Julie Super...

George comes in from the hall, talking

George It's no good. We can't get her started. (*He sees Julie*) Oh, my God!

George turns and walks straight out again

Maggie smiles at Julie

Maggie That was George.
Julie Yes. I know.
Maggie You mean you've met him already?
Julie Oh, yes. In here just now. He's awfully nice.
Maggie Yes, he is, isn't he?
Julie You're a very lucky woman.
Maggie (*puzzled*) Am I? Oh, good. I wasn't sure...

George comes back in, smiling sheepishly

George Sorry about that. Had to see to something in the hall. I didn't want him coming in here.
Julie Who?
George Er—big ginger cat on the landing! Huge! (*He demonstrates a big ginger cat*)
Maggie I didn't realize that you'd already *met* Julie.
George (*at a loss for a moment*) Julie? (*He realizes*) Oh—*this* Julie! Yes, she ... she did pop in for a moment.
Maggie And you met *him*, as well?

Act I, Scene 1 17

George Who?
Maggie Julie's boyfriend!

George looks blank

George Did I?
Maggie Well, he was here just now.
George Was he? (*Then he remembers*) Ah. Yes. Of course he was. I'd forgotten for a minute. Yes. Very nice chap. About so high. (*He indicates a man of rather small stature*)
Julie (*giggling*) What?!

George hastily adjusts the height to a much taller man

Maggie What's his height got to do with it?
George I don't know...
Julie Quite a coincidence, wasn't it, George?
George What was?
Julie You and he being old friends.
George (*smiling nervously*) Ah—yes, that *was* funny, wasn't it?
Maggie You mean ... *you* knew Julie's boyfriend *before*?
George (*thinking hard*) Er—yes. I *think* so.
Julie (*to Maggie*) They're old friends. Known each other for years.
Maggie Well, that certainly *is* a coincidence.
Julie (*to George*) I was just admiring her paintings.

George moves gratefully away from Maggie's questioning eyes

George Oh. On the walls? Yes. Very nice. Very nice indeed. (*Knowingly*) That's a calendar from the Express Dairy.
Julie You must be very proud of her.
George What? Ah! Yes! I'm always glad when Maggie paints. (*He puts a husbandly arm around Maggie, who is somewhat surprised*)
Julie Do you prefer her water colours or her oils?
Maggie He wouldn't know if I was painting in emulsion. (*She moves out of George's clutches*)
George Yes, I would! You'd use a roller.
Julie We'll have such a lot to talk about during dinner tonight.
George (*alarmed*) Dinner?
Maggie Yes. Julie's bringing her boyfriend over to dinner tonight.
George Oh, my God...!
Maggie George!
George Sorry, I...

Julie If it's not convenient...
Maggie It's perfectly convenient. We shall be delighted to see you. George has left his manners in the hall.
George (*quietly*) And that's not all! (*To Julie*) Does your boyfriend know he's coming to dinner tonight?
Julie Not yet. It'll be a nice surprise for him.
George It certainly will!
Maggie Perhaps *you*'d better stay for dinner, George?
George What?

Julie looks puzzled

Maggie As you're such old friends.
Julie Were you going out somewhere, then?
George Well, I...
Maggie You *can* stay, can't you?
Julie I don't want to upset your plans.
Maggie You won't do that. He can finish off the whisky.
George I'll need to!
Maggie That's settled, then. (*To Julie*) They can talk about the old days.
Julie Super...! I'd better go and finish unpacking or I shan't have a thing to wear tonight. (*She makes for the hall*)

George gently but firmly catches her arm as she passes and pivots her round in the opposite direction

George Not that way—this way!
Julie Of course. I forgot. We don't want to ruin your reputation, do we, George?

Julie grins at George, knowingly, and runs out into the garden

George laughs weakly and turns to see Maggie looking at him, suspiciously

Maggie I thought you said you hadn't met Julie's boyfriend.
George I'd forgotten!
Maggie Forgotten an "old friend"? Anyway, you'd better phone Brenda.
George Who?
Maggie Your wife!
George Oh, yes. Why?
Maggie (*as if to a child*) To let her know that you won't be home to dinner.
George Ah. Yes. Right. (*He sets off towards the telephone*)
Maggie Where did you know each other, then?

Act I, Scene 1   19

George (*stopping*) Who?
Maggie You and Phil and... Good heavens, she never told me his name.
George Whose name?
Maggie Julie's boyfriend's name! What is it?
George Ah—yes—now what is it...? (*He thinks hard*)
Maggie I thought you were old friends.
George That was a long time ago. You can't expect me to remember *every*thing!
Maggie His *name*, surely?
George His name, surely... Er—Alfred! Yes, that was it! (*Losing heart*) I think. Alfred something or other.

Mrs Puffet comes in briskly with her hat on

Puffet Two strong men and they can't get me going. So I'll have to be away.
Maggie Oh, must you?
Puffet Got to think of my husband's requirements, haven't I?
George In the middle of the p.m.?
Puffet He can't do without it, you know. And if I don't hurry up he won't get it.
George Get what?
Puffet His steak and kidney!
George (*grinning*) Oh, I see...!
Puffet Don't suppose anyone feels like running me down to the shops? On account of *someone* banging into my banger's backside. (*She looks, accusingly, at George*)

George sidles, guiltily, towards the drinks cupboard

Maggie Yes, of course, Mrs Puffet. I'll take you. Actually, I was wondering if you could possibly come back tonight.
Puffet Back here?
Maggie We're having people in to dinner. I could do with some help.
Puffet Oh, I don't know about that...
Maggie I would be grateful.
Puffet What about my husband's requirements?
Maggie Couldn't you leave him something frozen?
Puffet (*doubtfully*) Well...
Maggie Just this once.
Puffet Oh, all right, then.
Maggie Fine! I'll drop you at the shops.

Maggie and Mrs Puffet go out into the hall

George has arrived at the drinks cupboard and starts to pour himself a whisky

Phil comes in from the garden

Phil George!

George nearly spills his whisky

George Don't do that! I could have spilt the whisky.
Phil Has Maggie gone?
George Yes. She's dropping Mrs Puffet at the shops.
Phil Thank God for that! I'd better have one of those.
George Good idea. (*He pours another whisky*)

Phil sinks disconsolately on to the sofa

Phil Poor Julie's rattling around next door in an empty house. They've left it all unfurnished.
George She said she was going to unpack.
Phil George, there's nowhere to *put* anything!

George arrives with their drinks and sits next to Phil, who accepts the whisky gratefully

Cheers!
George Cheers!
Phil We'll have to pinch some furniture from here when Maggie isn't looking.
George You reckon?
Phil This is all *your* fault, you know!
George Yes. I thought it would be.
Phil You should have told Maggie right away.
George That you wanted a divorce? Not likely! Anyhow, by the time Maggie came home I'd already become the owner of this house and Julie thought Maggie was mine and not yours.
Phil Well, you'll have to sort *something* out, George. We can't leave it like this.
George (*casually*) Perhaps we can discuss it over dinner tonight.
Phil Yes. (*He reacts*) What?

George turns to Phil with a big smile

George Of course! You don't know, do you?

Act I, Scene 1

Phil Don't know what?
George You're coming to dinner tonight!
Phil Where?
George Here.
Phil What?!
George You and Julie are coming to dinner with you and Maggie.
Phil What are you talking about?
George Maggie asked Julie to dinner and to bring her boyfriend. That's you, isn't it?
Phil (*appalled*) And Julie said yes?
George Why shouldn't she? She thinks *you're* both coming to dinner with Maggie and *me*!
Phil Oh, my God...!

Julie comes in from the garden. She is not looking too pleased

Julie There's nothing to sit on!
Phil Isn't there?
Julie You said you'd get a sofa from somewhere.
Phil Yes, I did, didn't I? (*Quietly*) That was stupid of me...
Julie All there is is a drinks cabinet and a telly.
George What more do you want? (*He takes a big sip of whisky*)
Julie This is a fine start, isn't it?
Phil Is it? Oh, good!
Julie Already you're breaking promises.
Phil No, I'm not.
Julie What about the sofa, then?
Phil Ah. Yes. Er—it's here! (*He goes to the sofa, enthusiastically*)
Julie Where?
Phil Here! This is it!
Julie ⎫
George ⎭ (*together*) *This* one?
Phil It's a very nice sofa.
Julie Yes. But it's George's.
Phil No, it isn't. It's mine. Ours.
Julie Yours and mine?
Phil Yes.
Julie What's it doing here?
Phil It was delivered here by mistake. When the men arrived, this front door was open and they came straight in.
Julie Just like we did.
Phil Exactly! Easy thing to do. Easy mistake to make. Imagine my surprise when I came in here—to see George—and there was my sofa!

Julie Well—where's George's sofa?
Phil Gone to the cleaners.

George chokes on his drink

Julie (*astonished*) The *cleaners*?
Phil Yes. Too big for the launderette. (*To George, amused by the idea*) Just imagine it. Spinning round and round and round... (*He chuckles*)
Julie Phil!
Phil Yes?
Julie Why did George send his sofa to the cleaners?
Phil I dunno. Better ask him. It's his sofa. (*He grins at George, passing the buck*)
George I dropped the ketchup.
Phil He's a very messy eater.
Julie (*looking around*) It's going to look awfully bare in here without a sofa.
Phil (*fearfully*) Is it?
George Yes, it is!
Phil Well, he can bring something in from the garden.
George The mowing machine?
Phil Yes. Something like that.
Julie Will you bring it now?
Phil The mowing machine?
Julie The sofa!
Phil Ah. Yes, of course. Come on, George! (*Quietly*) Before she gets back!
George What?
Phil It's not very far to the shops!
Julie (*puzzled*) Shops?
Phil You go and open the door, darling. We'll come through this way.
Julie OK. Super!

Julie giggles and runs out into the garden

Phil and George prepare to lift the sofa

Phil Right. Here we go again. Do you prefer backwards or forwards?
George Oh, backwards, I think. I'd rather see where I've been than where I'm going.

Phil and George carry the sofa into the garden

Maggie comes in from the hall. She does not yet notice the absence of the sofa. She carries some shopping and two bottles of wine which she takes into the kitchen

Act I, Scene 1

A man comes quickly in from the hall. He is dressed in the uniform of an officer in the Fire Brigade. His name is Brasset

Maggie returns from the kitchen and sees yet another stranger standing in her sitting-room! She stops in surprise

Maggie Don't tell me I've parked on a double yellow line.
Brasset I'm not a traffic warden! I'm a fireman!
Maggie (*alarmed*) Good heavens! Is the house on fire?
Brasset Oh, no!
Maggie Oh, good!
Brasset But the front door was open so I came straight in.
Maggie I hope you haven't left your wet hose all over the carpet.
Brasset Oh, no. I haven't got it with me.
Maggie Then what are you doing here?
Brasset I'm looking for someone.
Maggie Anyone in particular?
Brasset Well, Julie, of course!
Maggie Julie? (*She jumps to the wrong conclusion*) Oh, I see! Then you must be... Good heavens, I'm so sorry! You aren't quite what we were expecting.
Brasset (*puzzled*) You *knew* I was coming?
Maggie Of course! Julie told me all about you.
Brasset Oh, dear. And I thought it was going to be a surprise...
Maggie (*reassuringly*) Well, it was a *bit*. She didn't say you'd be in uniform. And it's very smart. Very smart indeed. Do sit down. (*She indicates the place where the sofa used to be and sees for the first time that it is missing*) How extraordinary... There was a sofa here a *moment* ago. Where *can* it have got to? (*She glances about, deeply puzzled*)

Poor Mr Brasset looks more and more bewildered by this strange lady

Oh, well, never mind. It's bound to turn up sooner or later. (*She brings the desk chair down to where the sofa has been*) Here you are. You'd better sit on this.

Brasset looks at the chair without enthusiasm

Brasset Thank you. (*He sits, uncomfortably, on the chair*)

Maggie smiles broadly at him

Maggie Well—let me be the first to congratulate you!

Brasset Thank you. That's very kind. It *is* a bit of an honour.
Maggie (*puzzled*) Sorry?
Brasset I only became an officer a week ago. That's why I'm wearing the uniform, I suppose. (*He smiles, modestly*)
Maggie I meant congratulations about Julie.
Brasset Julie? Oh, well, I've got used to her by *now*! She's been around quite a long time, hasn't she? (*He laughs at his little joke*)
Maggie I thought you hadn't known her very long.
Brasset (*puzzled again*) I beg your pardon?
Maggie Anyway, I hope you'll be very happy living next door with Julie.
Brasset Oh, I shan't be *living* with her! (*He laughs at the idea*)
Maggie I thought you were just moving in?
Brasset She won't want *me* around the place all the time! I'll just call in occasionally to visit.
Maggie Good heavens, that's a *very* modern idea...
Brasset I'm so glad you were able to come in and get the place all ready. (*He reaches for his wallet*) Now how much do we owe you?
Maggie Sorry?
Brasset You *are* the cleaning lady?
Maggie No, I am not! Actually, Mr ... er...?
Brasset Brasset.
Maggie Mr Brasset, this is my house.
Brasset *Your* house? But I thought... This *is* number six, isn't it?
Maggie No. Number four. Number six is next door.
Brasset (*embarrassed*) Oh, dear me! I'm ever so sorry. I thought this was it. And seeing the front door open and welcome on the mat so to speak, I...
Maggie Came straight in.
Brasset Precisely.

Phil and George come in from the garden. They react at the sight of a strange man in a uniform sitting on a hard chair in the middle of the room

Phil Good God, it's the Police!
Brasset No, no! (*Proudly*) Fire Brigade.
Phil Oh, yes. It is different.

Maggie smiles at Phil and George, enthusiastically

Maggie He's put his uniform on specially.
Phil (*impressed*) He hasn't, has he? Did you hear that, George? He's put that lot on specially. (*To Brasset*) Very nice of you.
Maggie He's only been an officer a week.
Phil Never. Did you hear that, George? He's only been an officer a week.

Act I, Scene 1   25

George Doesn't show.
Phil No.
George Wouldn't have guessed.
Phil No. Turn around.

Obediently, Mr Brasset revolves

   Yes. Very good fit. Like a pair of rubber gloves.
Maggie Does Julie know he's here?
Phil (*puzzled*) Julie?
Maggie She didn't see him arrive?
Phil I don't think so.
Maggie Well, you'd better go and tell her.
Phil I expect she's seen a fireman before.
Brasset No, no! Don't tell her. I'll go round and surprise her.
Phil Surprise her? You'll frighten her to death!
Maggie Don't be silly. She'll be thrilled to see him.
Phil Will she?
Maggie Of course!
Phil I didn't know she had a passion for uniform.
Maggie Don't take any notice of him, Mr Brasset.
Phil Brasset? (*To George*) *I* know someone called Brasset...
Maggie I bet you're delighted to see him again, aren't you, Phil?
Phil Am I?
Maggie Yes, of course you are!
Phil Oh, all right. If you say so. Delighted to see you, Mr Brasset. (*He shakes the bewildered Brasset by the hand*)
Maggie Don't be so formal, for heaven's sake. You didn't call him Mr Brasset in the old days.
Phil Didn't I? (*To George*) What's she talking about?
George I've no idea!
Maggie Surely you remember the old days?
Phil No!
Maggie *You* remember them, don't you, George?
George (*uncertainly*) Do I?
Maggie And I'm sure you didn't call him Mr Brasset *then*.
Phil (*to George, bewildered*) I didn't call him *any*thing.
Maggie Don't say you've forgotten?
Phil Yes. Everything. Total blank.
Maggie (*to Brasset*) They forget things so easily. I was asking George about you earlier...
Brasset (*puzzled*) Were you?
Phil (*to George*) Was she?

George I didn't *think* so...
Maggie And it took him simply ages to remember your name.
George (*realizing*) Oh, my God...!
Brasset Percy.
Maggie What?
Brasset That's my name.
Maggie Percy?
Brasset Yes.
Maggie No. Alfred.
Brasset What?
Maggie Alfred.
Brasset Percy.
Maggie George!
Phil That's *your* name.
George I wish it wasn't!
Maggie George—it's Percy!
George Well, it was a long time ago. I must have forgotten. (*To Phil*) I think I'm going to faint.
Brasset I'll go and find Julie. (*He gets up*)
Phil You'd better sit down.
Brasset I've only just got up.
Phil Not you! George!

Brasset takes his chair back to the desk

George What?
Phil Sit down!
Maggie He can't. The sofa's gone.

Phil overdoes his assumption of surprise

Phil What?!
Maggie You didn't take it out into the garden, did you?
Phil No, of course not!
Brasset I'd better go and find Julie. (*He starts for the hall*)
Maggie Well, what's happened to it, then?
Phil The cleaners! They took it.
Maggie (*astonished*) The *cleaners*?!
Brasset Do you mind if I use the front door?
Maggie No. Sit down! (*She puts Brasset firmly into an armchair and turns to Phil*) Why should the cleaners take it?
Phil It was covered in ketchup.
George Yes. Red.

Act I, Scene 1   27

Brasset (*rising, alarmed*) Fire?
Maggie Be quiet!

Brasset sits again, abruptly

Phil So they came to the door in a van and took it away.
Maggie Well, what are we going to do?
Phil There are plenty of seats in the garden.
Maggie We shan't *be* in the garden!
Phil Bring them in.
Maggie Tubular chairs? We're having people to dinner!
Phil Well, ring them up and put them off!
Brasset (*rising*) Can I go now?
Maggie No. Sit down!

Brasset sits again

We can't put them off. It's so rude. (*To Brasset, with a smile*) We'll see you later, then, Alfred.
Brasset Percy!
Maggie You're coming to dinner tonight.
Phil ⎫ (*together*) What?
George ⎭
Brasset (*rising, astonished*) Here?
Maggie Yes.
Phil (*to George*) I've never had dinner with a fireman. Every time we strike a match he'll be reaching for the soda syphon. Why's he coming to dinner?
Maggie Don't be silly, Phil. He's Julie's.
Phil Julie's?
Maggie Yes. You know!
Brasset I don't know that I can stay.
Phil Thank God for that!
Brasset I might get called out.
George Yes. London could be ablaze.
Maggie But this is an important night for you, Alfred.
All Percy!
Maggie The first night in your little nest. I know you're not married yet, but it's the permissive age and we're all broadminded.
Brasset (*outraged*) Now, look here, I may only be a fireman but I do know what's what!
Phil Well, that's more than I do.
Maggie You mean it isn't true?
Brasset I'd like to find the person who told you! I'll have you know, I'm a respectable man.

George Then what the hell are you doing *here*?
Maggie We'll see you later, then, Percy?
Brasset I'll have to ask *her*.
Maggie Oh, she's already accepted.

Julie runs in from the garden

Brasset sees her and smiles, delightedly

Brasset Julie!

Julie sees him and beams with joy

Julie What a wonderful surprise! (*She runs across to Brasset*)

Phil and George look astonished

Phil You mean you really *know* this fireman?
Julie Of course I know him. (*She links hands with Brasset affectionately*) I know him and I love him!
Phil }
George } (*together*) What?!
Brasset Julie!
Julie Daddy!

Julie and her father embrace. Maggie looks at them in surprise. Phil and George look at each other in alarm

Phil }
George } (*together*) Daddy?!

They embrace

Black-out

Music plays until...

Scene 2

Later the same evening; pleasant summer sunshine filtering through the windows

Maggie is coming in from the garden, wearing a towelling bathrobe and carrying two tubular garden chairs

She erects them in the space left by the vacant sofa, tries to arrange them attractively but is not too happy about the result

Mrs Puffet bustles in from the hall with her hat on

Puffet He didn't like it.
Maggie (*engrossed in her chairs*) H'm?
Puffet Me here and him there. It's not what he fancies. (*She goes to fold up one of the garden chairs*) The place for these is in the shed.
Maggie There are people coming to dinner! (*She opens the chair up again*)
Puffet I know. So you get yourself ready, dear, and I'll put these back where they belong. (*She starts to fold up the second chair*)
Maggie (*restraining her*) But there's nowhere for them to sit! (*She opens the chair up again*)
Puffet What?
Maggie Hadn't you noticed?

Mrs Puffet notices

Puffet Here! Who's pinched your sofa?
Maggie My husband sent it to the cleaners.
Puffet (*doubtfully*) Oh, yes?
Maggie Well, that's what he *said*.
Puffet Been working too hard, I suspect.
Maggie So we'll have to use these. (*She adjusts the position of the chairs a little*)
Puffet What about the armchair in your bedroom? We could bring that down.
Maggie I thought of that but it seems to have disappeared.
Puffet Disappeared?
Maggie While I was in the bath.
Puffet Hasn't sent that to the cleaners, too, has he?
Maggie I hope not. And now he and George have vanished as well.
Puffet Something funny about them two, if you ask me. They've been acting very furtive this p.m.
Maggie *You* noticed that, too?

Puffet Oh, yes. Very furtive. (*She makes for the kitchen*)
Maggie (*thoughtfully*) By the way, that old wardrobe in the spare room—we didn't send it to the jumble sale, did we?
Puffet No. The Boy Scouts was coming with their van but they never showed up.

Mrs Puffet disappears into the kitchen

Maggie (*thoughtfully*) That's what I thought...

Maggie goes out into the hall

The moment she has gone, Phil and George come in from the garden. They are breathless, and George is holding a painful back

George I think I've done something dreadful. I'm not supposed to be a furniture remover!
Phil Do stop fussing. They were only little things.
George You can't call that wardrobe a little thing! (*He sinks into one of the garden chairs, exhausted*) You don't suppose Maggie saw us, do you?
Phil She was in the bath. She couldn't see us from there. (*Amused*) I wonder what the neighbours thought...
George Never mind what the neighbours thought! What's Maggie going to think when she finds her bedroom chair missing?
Phil You don't know Maggie. She won't even notice that it's gone.
George Want a bet?
Phil Well, I couldn't leave poor Julie all unfurnished, could I? (*He sits beside George in the other chair*)

They stare ahead, bleakly, looking rather incongruous sitting side-by-side on two garden chairs as though they were on the beach. After a moment, Phil chuckles at his own thoughts

You know, somehow I never thought I'd have a fireman for a father-in-law. I wonder what it'll be like...
George (*casually*) Well, you'll find out over dinner tonight.

Phil remembers with alarm

Phil Oh, my God! I'd forgotten all about this wretched dinner party! What am I going to do? How can I be Maggie's husband *and* Julie's boyfriend both at the same time?
George You should have thought of that before and kept off the 49 bus.

Act I, Scene 2   31

Phil (*dreamily*) I'm a romantic, George. I just couldn't resist her…
George You can't resist *any* of them!
Phil She wore a little yellow hat and grey boots…
George Is that all? Must have been rather conspicuous.
Phil (*ignoring this*) I sat down next to her and instantly I knew that we had something in common…
George Why? Were *you* wearing a yellow hat as well?
Phil I knew at once that this was going to be the big thing in my life…
George Well, next time take a taxi and settle for the little things.

Maggie comes in from the hall. She is now wearing a dress. She sees George and Phil sitting on the garden chairs

Maggie Good heavens, you both look exhausted! Don't tell me *you*'ve been taking some exercise?
George Yes—just a little…! (*He gives Phil a look*)
Maggie Well, you'd better freshen up before all these guests arrive.

Maggie goes into the kitchen

Phil looks at George in panic

Phil Oh, my God…!

Phil gets up and goes towards the kitchen, anxiously, and meets Maggie as she returns, putting on an apron

Now, Maggie—about this dinner party. The thing is——
Maggie Fancy Mr Brasset being Julie's father! I thought he was her boyfriend. Poor man. He must have been so embarrassed. (*She starts putting out various dishes of nuts and Twiglets*) Anyway, I've told Mrs Puffet to lay an extra place.
Phil No!
Maggie (*surprised by his vehemence*) What?
Phil I—I don't think this dinner party's a very good idea.
Maggie But I've got Mrs Puffet specially. Besides, I've asked them now.
Phil (*hopefully*) Perhaps they can't come?
Maggie They *can* come. They've accepted.
Phil But *he*'s not *here*!
Maggie Who?
Phil Him! The boyfriend! Julie's!
Maggie He was just now.
Phil Was he?

Maggie Well, I saw people next door.
Phil (*nervously*) Did you?
Maggie Yes.
George I thought you were in your bath.
Maggie When I got *out* of my bath.
Phil Er—anyone you recognized?
Maggie Well, I couldn't see them very clearly.
Phil (*quietly*) Thank God for that...!
Maggie Sorry?
George They were delivery men! Delivering things. And now they've left.
Phil And *he* hasn't *arrived*!
Maggie Julie's boyfriend?
Phil Probably lost on the motorway.
Maggie Don't be silly. He's already *been* here.
Phil Has he?
Maggie Of course he has! You both spoke to him in here. Didn't you, George?
George Well, *I* did. I don't know about Phil. (*He looks at Phil, uncertainly*)
Phil Ah—yes, but then he had to go again.
Maggie Why?
Phil He'd left something behind. So he dashed off to get it.
Maggie Then he'll soon be back.
Phil Possibly, but not in time for dinner.
Maggie Well, we shall *wait* dinner for him, won't we?
Phil Will we?
Maggie Of course! It would be very rude to start without him. We can all have drinks until he arrives.
George (*quietly, to Phil*) We'll be well away by then!
Maggie I'm really looking forward to tonight. It'll be nice to meet new people.
Phil Yes, it would. I mean—yes, it will!
Maggie It's just such a pity that you chose today to send the sofa to be cleaned. (*She gives him an old-fashioned look*)
Phil Well, I didn't know that you were going to invite two perfect strangers to dinner!
George Three.
Phil What?
George Don't forget the fireman.
Maggie By the way, what happened to the armchair?
Phil (*nervously*) Er ... armchair?
Maggie In our bedroom.
Phil Ah—yes—there *was* an armchair there, wasn't there?
Maggie And now there isn't.

Act I, Scene 2   33

George I didn't think she'd notice. Did you, Phil? (*He grins at Phil*)

Phil glares at him and then turns back to Maggie and tries to carry it off

Phil I thought it was a nice friendly gesture. Poor Julie. Great big house and nowhere to sit. I felt a bit mean.
Maggie So you lent her our bedroom chair?
Phil Yes...
Maggie And the old wardrobe, as well?
Phil That was going to the Boy Scouts, anyway!
Maggie I see. And what *other* things of mine is Julie going to borrow?

Julie runs in from the garden. Her dress is unzipped at the back

Julie You keep disappearing! Will you please come and help me get dressed?

They all look at her. Quite a pause. Phil turns slowly to look at George, passing the buck. George sees Phil looking at him, realizes what he is up to and turns away. Phil leans slowly across and reaches out to George, trying to attract his attention. As if by radar, George senses the approaching hand and slowly angles his body out of reach. Finally...

Phil George... I think she's talking to you.
George (*apprehensively*) Is she?
Julie I can never manage the last bit of my zip.
Phil George!
George What?
Phil Pay attention. Julie wants her zip done up.

Deeply embarrassed, George rises reluctantly and goes across to Julie. He fastens her dress. Julie, naturally, is a little surprised!

Julie Oh—well, thank you, George. But I was really meaning——
Phil (*quickly*) He's very good at them. Had plenty of practice.
Julie Oh, yes, of course. I expect he's always zipping *your* dresses up and down, Maggie.
Maggie Only when he's very drunk.

Julie goes to Phil

Julie You'd better hurry up if you're going to have a bath.

Maggie looks surprised

Phil (*nervously*) A ... a bath?
Julie Before dinner. You are going to have one, aren't you?
Phil Er ... yes ... I suppose so.
Maggie Of course you are, Phil. You'd better pop upstairs now before it gets cold. I ran it for you ten minutes ago.

It is Julie's turn to look surprised

Julie That's very kind of you, Maggie. But he can easily have a bath next door.
Maggie (*puzzled*) In *your* house?
Julie Why not?
Maggie Oh, you wouldn't want Phil trundling all over your bathroom when you've only just moved in. Another time, perhaps.
George Yes. He's very messy in the bathroom. Splashes about like a porpoise.
Maggie Besides, I've put the bubble bath in all ready for him.
Julie Oh. Oh, well, that's very kind of you. I'll just go and get him a towel. (*She starts to go*)
Maggie A *towel*?
Julie It's the least I can do.
Maggie It's very kind of you to offer. But you don't have to worry. We've got plenty of towels upstairs.
Julie Is ... is that all right with you, then, Phil?
Phil Oh, yes. I'm quite happy to bath here. Make a change.
Maggie What?
Phil From the morning! I usually bath in the morning!
Julie It does seem a pity, though.
Maggie What does?
Julie Well .. *I've* run a bath, too.
George Very clean people in the suburbs.
Julie Seems such a shame to waste it.
Maggie Yes, it does, doesn't it? (*She turns slowly and looks across at George*) George...

George reacts in alarm

...couldn't *you* have a bath next door?
George What on earth for?
Maggie Well, Phil's bathing here so there's no room for you.
George I don't want a bath!
Phil Oh, yes, you do! You're not eating here all unwashed and unbrushed!
Julie You're very welcome, George. If you'd like to.

Act I, Scene 2   35

Maggie But wait a minute, Julie—what about your...?
Phil (*quickly*) Yes! Doesn't *he* want a bath?
Julie I don't expect so. He likes to keep his clothes on in case there's an emergency.
Maggie Really? Oh, well, that's all settled, then. Phil, you're bathing here. George, you're bathing next door, and I'll go and fetch you a towel. (*She starts for the hall*)
Julie You needn't bother. There are plenty of Phil's towels next door. (*She looks, thoughtfully, at the two garden chairs*)

Maggie stops and turns to look at Phil in surprise

Maggie What on earth are your towels doing next door?
Phil Er—wedding present.
Maggie A bit premature.
Phil I always was impetuous.
Julie (*staring at the garden chairs*) It does look a bit odd without the sofa, doesn't it?
Maggie Yes, it does...
Phil No, it doesn't! (*He goes, enthusiastically, to the garden chairs*) Nothing wrong with these chairs. Good solid garden chairs. We can imagine we're in the South of France. Or Italy. Somewhere like that. Out in the sun, soaking it up. Shining with Ambre Solaire and watching the world go by!
Maggie But we shan't be. We're having dinner, not going on a package holiday. And I may be old-fashioned but in a house I do prefer a sofa to a couple of tubular chairs.
Julie I've got a wonderful idea!
George (*to Phil*) She wants us *all* to have a bath next door!
Phil What a splendid thought! All bobbing about like a football team.

The men laugh together

Julie I'll lend you *my* sofa.

The men stop laughing

Maggie Oh, I couldn't ask you to do that.
Phil No, of course you couldn't!
Julie (*to Maggie*) Well, *we* shan't be using it tonight because we shall be over here.
Maggie Oh, no. It would be too much trouble.
Julie No. Phil and George can carry it through the garden.
Maggie But it might not go through that doorway.

Julie Yes, it does! It goes quite easily.
Maggie Does it?
Julie Oh, yes.
Maggie How do you know?
Julie Well, because——
Phil It's the same as next door! They're identical.
Julie And they managed before.
Maggie Who did?
Phil The men! Two men! Huge men in caps!
Maggie (*to Julie*) Well—in that case perhaps it would be nice. If you're sure you don't mind.
Julie Of course I don't mind. It'll be a little way that I can repay you for *your* kindness.
Maggie (*modestly*) Yes. After all, I did lend you my bedroom chair, didn't I?

Julie looks puzzled and turns to Phil

Julie Phil...?
Phil I'd better go and have my bath or there'll be bubbles all over the landing. (*He starts to go*)
Julie You'd better move the sofa first.
Phil Ah. Yes. (*He looks at the garden chairs*) I do *like* these chairs, don't you, George?
George Yes. Nice class of chair...
Julie The sofa!
Phil The sofa. Yes. Right. Come on, George.

Phil and George go towards the garden. They hesitate for a moment

   Of course, there is one boring thing about sofas. They do all look alike, don't they?

Getting no response, Phil and George stumble out into the garden

Maggie and Julie start to fold up the garden chairs

Maggie Sweet boys!
Julie Yes. It'll be lovely having George living next door to us.
Maggie (*surprised*) I didn't know George was moving.
Julie Oh, I don't mean George is moving. I mean us moving in next door to George.

Maggie tries to understand

Act I, Scene 2

Maggie You mean you're moving out again so soon? You've only just moved in! You don't believe in putting down roots, do you? Travelling from place to place all the time.
Julie (*confused*) I don't quite follow...
Maggie Perhaps your father's got gypsy blood?
Julie Sorry?
Maggie That would account for his adventurous spirit, wouldn't it? Joining the Fire Service and all that.
Julie Oh, no. He just likes bonfires.
Maggie (*bemused*) I see. Anyway, I'm glad he's coming to dinner tonight.
Julie My father?
Maggie I did invite him.
Julie That was kind of you, but he's really only at home in a fire station.
Maggie A pity we haven't got red wallpaper. (*She laughs at her little joke*) Anyway, Alfred will be here to keep him company.
Julie Alfred?
Maggie He will be *back* in time, won't he?
Julie (*puzzled*) Who's Alfred?
Maggie Don't tell me I've got *his* name wrong, as well?
Julie Whose name?
Maggie Your boyfriend's name.
Julie His name's not Alfred!
Maggie Isn't it?
Julie No.
Maggie Second name, perhaps?

Phil and George come in, carrying the sofa

Phil Where would you like us to put it? Here—or here?

They deliberately try to put it away from its usual place

Maggie Oh, the usual place, I think.
Phil The usual place, George.
George Usual place...

They reluctantly put it down in its usual place

Julie There! That looks better, doesn't it?

Maggie comes across, intrigued, peering at the sofa carefully. The men wait for the balloon to go up

Maggie Well...! It shows what a lot we have in common, doesn't it, Julie?

Julie Oh?
Maggie Choosing identical sofas!

The men relax

Now you really must go and have your bath, Phil. Those bubbles will be halfway down the stairs by now.
Phil Ah. Yes. Right.
George And I'll have mine.

Phil and George go quickly in opposite directions

Julie Phil! Would you like me to come up and scrub your back?

They all react. A dreadful pause

Phil Oh, you don't have to do that!
Julie Why not?
Phil I've got a very long loofah.

Phil realizes what he has said and hastens into the hall and up the stairs

George laughs. Julie turns to look at him

George stops laughing and beats a hasty retreat into the garden

Julie turns to Maggie with a smile

Julie You're very lucky being married to someone like George.
Maggie Oh, do you think they're *alike*?
Julie He's very sweet.
Maggie Yes, isn't he?
Julie Well, I'll just go and get a towel for George.

Julie goes out into the garden

Maggie looks puzzled

Mrs Puffet comes in from the kitchen, severely

Puffet What is it, then? Five or six for dinner?
Maggie Ah. Let me see now ... four for certain, probably five, but six if the fireman turns up.

Act I, Scene 2   39

Puffet (*heavily*) In that case I'd better do another potato. The rest'll have to spread. (*She sees the sofa*) That didn't take long at the cleaners.
Maggie Oh, that's not *our* sofa.
Puffet Looks just like it.
Maggie Yes, that's what *I* thought. But one of our guests has *lent* it to us for the evening.
Puffet (*doubtfully*) Oh, yes? A likely tale!

Mrs Puffet goes into the kitchen, giving the sofa a suspicious glance as she passes

Maggie takes the garden chairs outside

Greta strides in from the hall, looking about. She is very pretty. She is also extremely angry

Maggie returns from the garden

Greta (*abruptly*) All right! Where is he?

Maggie is astonished to find yet another stranger in her sitting-room

Maggie Sorry?
Greta You wait till I find him!
Maggie (*puzzled*) What makes you think you'll find him *here*?
Greta This *is* number four, isn't it?
Maggie Yes, but——
Greta That's what I thought! And the front door was open——
Maggie So you came straight in?
Greta Well, the bell isn't working!
Maggie I'm sorry. I'll get a man to fix it in the morning.
Greta I'm really fed up with him! (*She flings herself down on the sofa, angrily*)
Maggie Yes. I can see that you are. You wanted to *tell* someone about it, is that it?
Greta Oh, no—I mustn't interrupt your work. I can see you're busy. (*She indicates Maggie's apron*)
Maggie Sorry? (*She looks down at her apron*)
Greta (*blazing*) He should have been with *me* tonight!
Maggie Really?
Greta He promised!
Maggie Oh, dear. Men are so thoughtless.
Greta I'd arranged dinner at home specially. He knew that! The pig!

Maggie Dinner at home...? (*She jumps to the wrong conclusion*) Oh, I see. So *that's* who you are! I'm so sorry. I didn't realize. Didn't he telephone you?
Greta No.
Maggie It's all my fault. I asked him to stay *here* for dinner. I thought it would be nice. As they all know each other so well. But I assumed he'd have rung you. I did ask him to.
Greta Well, he didn't!
Maggie He's so forgetful. Anyway, it's very nice to meet you at last. (*She holds out her hand*)
Greta (*puzzled*) Sorry?
Maggie And *you* must stay to dinner, too.
Greta What?
Maggie I insist!
Greta He is here, then?
Maggie Oh, yes. He's in the bath next door.

Greta is even more bewildered

Greta Trouble with the plumbing?
Maggie Sorry?
Greta Here.
Maggie Oh, no. Just a bit of a run on the bathroom. (*She takes off her apron*) Perhaps I'd better get you a drink. You look as if you need one.
Greta Yes, I do...!
Maggie So do I! (*She goes towards the drinks cupboard*) Vodka and tonic all right?
Greta Lovely. (*She feels embarrassed*) I'm afraid I've made a dreadful mistake...
Maggie Really?
Greta I thought you were the cleaning lady.

Maggie bears this with as much fortitude as she can muster

Maggie You're the second person who's thought that today.
Greta I'm sorry...
Maggie (*busy pouring the drinks*) It's funny, really, that we've never met before, isn't it?
Greta (*puzzled*) Is it?
Maggie With them being such old friends. It was such a pity that we couldn't get to the wedding, but it was rather sudden and we were away at the time. (*She arrives with the drinks*) Here we are.
Greta Thanks. (*She takes a generous sip, gratefully*)

Maggie notices this, but maintains her social graces

Maggie I've often suggested that he bring you over here, but he always has some excuse. (*She laughs*) I began to think his wife must have two heads or something, but you're very pretty. Cheers! (*She drinks*)
Greta Good heavens, I'm not his *wife*!
Maggie You're not?
Greta No! I'm just ... a friend.
Maggie (*realizing*) Oh, I *see*...!
Greta I didn't know he was married. Although when you said you weren't the cleaning lady I did wonder if *you*——
Maggie Oh, no! *I'm* just a friend, too.
Greta (*put out*) He never told me about *you*!
Maggie Sorry?
Greta Did he tell you about *me*?
Maggie No, he certainly didn't! He's kept you *very* secret. Well, well! The old dark horse. I can't tell you how surprised I am. I'd never have thought it of him. I mean—it's so unlike him! (*She chuckles, happily*)
Greta You're not angry, then?
Maggie What about?
Greta About *me*!
Maggie Why should I be angry? He's not my property! As far as I'm concerned he can do what he likes.
Greta Oh. That's all right, then. Here—you don't suppose his wife *knows* about us, do you?
Maggie Well, she knows about *me*.
Greta (*surprised*) Really?
Maggie Oh, yes. But I bet she doesn't know about *you*! (*She laughs*)
Greta (*fearfully*) She won't turn up here tonight, will she?
Maggie Why not? The party's getting bigger every minute!

Mrs Puffet comes in from the kitchen with a dish of nuts. She sees Greta

Puffet Don't say there's more!
Maggie Yes. I'm afraid you'll have to do another potato.
Puffet (*heavily*) My husband wasn't keen on me coming here in the first place. (*She plonks the nuts down on the table in front of Greta*)
Maggie No, I know he wasn't.
Puffet (*to Greta*) On account of his requirements.
Maggie (*going to pacify her*) Yes, and we're very grateful to you, Mrs Puffet. Very grateful. So if you wouldn't mind just laying another place. (*She ushers Mrs Puffet back towards the kitchen*)
Puffet (*beadily*) Any more and it'll have to be a take-away.

Mrs Puffet goes back into the kitchen

Maggie Her husband's very particular.
Greta I wouldn't have thought so…

George comes in from the garden

Maggie meets him with a broad smile

George I couldn't have a bath after all. That wretched fireman was already in it. (*He sees Maggie grinning at him*) What's the matter with you? You're grinning like a Cheshire cat.

Maggie takes his arm and leads him away, smiling at the thought of his guilty secret

Maggie You wicked old thing!
George What?
Maggie I would never have guessed. Whatever's Brenda going to say? (*She nudges him, playfully*)
George (*bewildered*) Sorry—I don't quite——
Maggie Haven't you noticed?
George What?
Maggie On the sofa…

George turns and sees a completely strange blonde sitting on the sofa. He turns back to Maggie, even more bewildered. She is still smiling hugely

George A girl.
Maggie Well, go and say hullo then!

George, puzzled, crosses to look more closely at Greta. He waves a paw, vaguely

George Hullo.
Greta (*puzzled*) Hullo…

George goes back to Maggie

George Who is it?
Maggie You don't have to pretend. I know all about her.
George Do you?
Maggie Yes.

Act I, Scene 2

George All?
Maggie Yes.
George Is that a lot?
Maggie It's enough!
George Oh. (*He glances briefly at Greta*) Very pretty.
Maggie Go and kiss her, then.
George What?!
Maggie Go on! *I* don't mind.
George *She* might.
Maggie Now you're being modest.
George I don't go around kissing ladies on sofas. Not unless I'm drunk.
Maggie Oh, you're shy, is that it? All right, then—I'll leave you two together. (*To Greta*) Isn't he sweet?

Maggie turns in the doorway, winks and clicks her tongue at George, and goes out giggling

George and Greta look at each other, totally bewildered by this extraordinary behaviour

Greta What was that all about?
George I've no idea! I *haven't* met you before, have I?
Greta No. I've only just arrived.
George Are you staying for dinner?
Greta Yes.
George So am I. It's going to be quite a party.
Greta How many of us will there be?
George I wish I knew! Either five or seven ... I *think*...
Phil (*off*) George! George!

Phil rushes in from the hall, chuckling happily. He goes to George, excitedly. He does not see Greta

I say—what's all this exciting news? Maggie says you've got yourself a girlfriend!
George Don't be ridiculous!
Phil That's what *I* said! (*He sees a girl on the sofa and grins at George, playfully*) George, you old devil! Well, come on—aren't you going to introduce us? (*Bubbling with joy, he crosses to Greta*)

Greta turns and glares at him, furiously

Greta All right, Phil—where *were* you?

Phil's face falls as he recognizes her

Phil Greta! What the hell are *you* doing here?

George looks alarmed

Black-out

CURTAIN

ACT II

The same. A few seconds later

They are in the same positions as before. Greta is glaring at Phil, furiously

Greta Well? Where were you?
Phil When?
Greta Tonight!
Phil I was here. With George.
Greta Well, you should have been with *me*!
Phil Should I?
Greta (*to George*) He was supposed to be having dinner with *me* tonight but he seems to have forgotten.
George Well, he has had other things on his mind…
Phil (*quietly*) Yes, and I wish I hadn't! (*To Greta*) Are you sure it was today?
Greta Yes! I wrote it down in my diary. We were meeting at six thirty.
Phil Were we?
Greta And you forgot! (*She pummels him on the chest*) I waited an hour for you to turn up.
Phil And I didn't?
Greta No! So I looked you up in the phone book and came straight round.
Phil And I bet the front door was open?
Greta Yes.
Phil Blast Mrs Puffet!
Greta (*turning to George*) You'll never guess where I met him.
George I bet *I will*…!
Greta (*romantically*) On top of a bus…
George Never!
Greta It was so romantic. Ducks on the pond, the sun shining. (*To Phil*) And you came and sat down beside me.
Phil (*laughing nervously*) Like a big spider.
George You don't seem to have frightened her away, though.

Phil glares at George

Greta (*angrily*) But you've forgotten all that now, haven't you?
Phil No, no—I remember the bus!

George I bet it was a number forty-nine...
Greta (*suspiciously*) Have you been telling him about me?
Phil Well, he *was* my best man.
Greta What?!
Phil I mean he is my best friend!

Greta pummels him on the chest again

Greta How could you forget all about me like that?
Phil Well, it was a long time ago.
Greta I expect you hoped that *I*'d forgotten all about it, as well?
Phil Yes.
Greta What?!
Phil No! No, of course not!
Greta You didn't *mean* it, then?
Phil Oh, yes. I meant it *then*.
Greta But you don't mean it *now*?
Phil Well—the thing is—it's the situation. It's changed a little.
George Yes. It is a bit fluid!
Greta Is it because of that other woman you've got in the house?
Phil Mrs Puffet?
Greta No. The *other* woman.
Phil Ah.

A moment's silence. The men think deeply

George What other woman?
Phil Thank you, George. That's just what I was thinking.
Greta I don't know her name but she talked about you.
Phil (*apprehensively*) Did she?
Greta Yes. *She*'s in the same position as *I* am.

Phil considers

Phil Er ... what position is that?
Greta Not married to you!
Phil (*thinking hard*) Two women in this house not married to me and one of them isn't Mrs Puffet...
George Narrows the field a bit.
Phil Two women in this house not married to me and... Good God! You've seen her!
Greta That's what I was trying to tell you.
Phil She's been in here!

Act II

Greta Yes.
Phil Talking to you!
Greta Yes.
Phil What about?
George About you, you fool!

Phil ambles away to look out into the garden, anxiously

Phil What did she say about me?
Greta She said she didn't mind.
Phil Didn't mind?
Greta That *I* was a girlfriend of yours, as well. She said as far as she was concerned you could do what you liked.

Phil is shattered

Phil She said that? Good heavens. Did you hear that, George?
George H'm?
Phil Oh, do pay attention! I'm disillusioned.
George I'm sorry. (*He hangs his head*)
Phil Not about you! About her. Shattered and disillusioned.
George And in trouble.
Phil What?
George She's coming across the garden!
Phil Oh, my God! George, you haven't shown Greta the upstairs.
George Haven't I?
Phil You'd better do it now.
George Well, I...
Phil There may not be another opportunity. (*He urges George and Greta towards the hall*)
Greta I don't want to go upstairs!
Phil Yes, you do. You've had a very long journey.

Phil pushes George and Greta out into the hall and closes the door after them

Julie comes in from the garden

Julie What was it like, darling?

Phil looks blank

Phil What?

Julie Having a bath in a strange house.
Phil Never mind about the bath.

He goes to her to ingratiate himself. He leads her by the hand to the sofa and they sit down, side-by-side

Look—it isn't true.
Julie Sorry?
Phil About that other woman. She doesn't mean a thing to me.
Julie Mrs Puffet?
Phil No, no! The other one.
Julie George's wife? I should hope not. You'll be in trouble if you mess about with Maggie.
Phil No, not Maggie! The other one!
Julie What other one? (*She watches him with growing surprise as he rattles on*)
Phil It was a passing acquaintance, that was all! So whatever she says it isn't true! There's no question of sharing. I'm going to marry *you*! It was sweet of you to say you didn't mind about her. But I *want* you to mind! It's important to *me* that you mind! (*He realizes how this sounds and hastily covers*) Even if there's nothing to mind about!
Julie What *are* you talking about?
Phil Sorry?
Julie Don't get so excited. (*She embraces him, fondly*) Calm down now. Just calm down. (*She kisses him*)

Mrs Puffet comes in with some more nuts and sees them

Puffet (*abruptly*) Nuts!
Phil What?
Puffet More nuts!
Phil We haven't finished the last lot yet.
Puffet Too busy, I suspect? Doing *other* things.
Phil Oh, that. That was nothing, Mrs Puffet.
Julie No. He can do much better than that. (*She cuddles up to him, hopefully*)

Phil quickly extricates himself

Puffet (*to Julie, suspiciously*) You the new one, then? From next door?
Julie Yes. We moved in today.
Puffet Didn't take you long to get friendly with the neighbours.
Phil Ah—now don't misunderstand, Mrs Puffet! You see—it's my birthday. People have been kissing me all day. Every time I've walked down the

Act II

street strange people have stopped me and said "Happy birthday!" and given me a real smacker. Even the vicar. They've been at it all day. *You* wouldn't like to kiss me, would you, Mrs Puffet?

Puffet No fear!
Phil Please yourself. I'm only free today.
Puffet (*to Julie*) I hope you're not going to be like the last lot.
Julie Next door?
Puffet Drew their curtains and carried on.
Julie Of course not, Mrs Puffet. We're not like that, are we, Phil? (*She links her arm in his*)
Phil (*extricating himself*) Certainly not.
Puffet We shall see. Can't say I'm impressed by what I've seen so far.
Julie What?
Puffet I *was* going to offer you a couple of my p.ms but now I'm not so sure!

Mrs Puffet goes out in full sail, taking the nuts with her

Julie What's she talking about?
Phil Don't take any notice. She means well. She's only cross because we won't eat her nuts.
George (*off*) Wait a minute! You mustn't go down there!

Phil hears George and Greta returning, and he panics

Phil Oh, my God! They're coming back! Now remember—whatever she tells you, it isn't true!

Julie looks bewildered

Greta comes in from the hall, followed by a desperate George

What have *you* come back for?
Greta I need another voddie. (*She marches towards the drinks cupboard, but sees Julie on the sofa and stops, facing her in horror*) Oh, my God!
Phil What's the matter?
Greta You must be his wife!
Julie Wife? What wife? Phil...?
Phil She's a little confused. (*He turns to look at George*) George...!

George turns, apprehensively, and they look at each other

You're very quiet.
George I'm writing a poem.

Greta (*to Julie*) I only hope you're going to be as understanding about me as you are about the other one.
Julie What other one?
Greta I thought you'd be absolutely furious. After all, you can't have been married very long.
Julie I haven't been married at all!
Greta (*surprised*) You mean you're *not* married to him?
Julie No. Not yet.
Greta (*staring at her in disbelief*) And you still don't mind about the other one?

Julie goes to Phil, in a daze

Julie Phil...?
Phil Yes?
Julie What's she talking about?
Phil You know!
Julie No, I don't.
Phil Haven't you spoken to her before?
Julie I've never even seen her before!

Phil goes to Greta

Phil (*indicating Julie*) Isn't this the one you spoke to?
Greta Oh, no! It was somebody else.

Phil tramps across to George

Phil Oh, my God! There are *three* women in this house not married to me and two of them aren't Mrs Puffet! There's another one loose!
George I expect there's a 49 bus full of 'em outside!

Phil glares at him

Greta (*to Julie*) You do *live* here, though, don't you?
Julie No. I live next door. Number six.
Greta (*astonished*) You mean you don't even *live* together?
Phil (*to George*) We've got to get rid of her!
George Which one?
Phil The second one, you fool!
George Yes, of course. First come, first served.
Phil Go on, then!
George Why should *I* do all the dirty work?

Act II

Phil You came here to help!
George Well, I've carried that damn sofa in and out.
Phil Compared with the sofa, this is easy.
George *You* do it, then! (*He sits down, defiantly*)

Phil glares at him and then goes quickly across to Greta

Phil Come on!
Greta Where are we going?
Phil I'll show you the front door.
Greta I don't want to see your beastly front door. The bell doesn't work.
Phil Well, you can't stay here!
Greta Why not?
Phil Because there are people coming to dinner!
Greta Yes, I know. (*She turns to George*) How many did you say there were going to be, George? Five or seven, was it?

George cowers, nervously, as Phil comes towards him, seething

Phil Oh, you had a little conversation, then? Had a little chat?
George (*mumbling*) Just a brief ... er...
Phil Found something to say *then*! (*To Greta*) There's only four for dinner, as a matter of fact.
George Five.
Phil What?
George You've forgotten to count yourself.
Phil I *did* count myself.
George (*pointedly*) Once or twice?
Phil Ah—yes—I see what you mean. (*To Greta*) There are five for dinner.
Julie Five?
George And that's not counting the fireman.
Phil There are six for dinner! So there's no room for you. You'll have to go.
Greta But I tell you I've been invited!
Phil Never!
Greta When I arrived. She invited me. In fact, she insisted.
Phil She?
Greta The other one!

Maggie comes sailing in from the hall

Maggie Now, has everyone got a drink?
Greta I'd love another voddie.
Maggie George, aren't you looking after—er...?

Greta Greta.
Maggie Greta.
George Right, right, right… (*He shambles off to get more vodka for Greta*)

Phil takes Maggie aside a little and whispers to her

Phil Have you *really* invited her?
Maggie Who?
Phil Greta.
Maggie Yes, of course. It was the least I could do. George would have been very upset if I hadn't.
Phil Would he? (*He looks across at George, puzzled*)

George pours vodka liberally into a glass and hands it to Greta

Maggie (*to Phil*) I think he's got rather good taste.
Phil Who?
Maggie George!
Phil Has he?
Maggie I wonder what Brenda will say if she finds out.
Phil What's Brenda got to do with it?

Maggie crosses to Julie

Maggie Julie, you haven't got a drink. What would you like?
Julie Sherry, please.
George (*abruptly*) All right! All right! I'll get it! I'll get it! (*He pours sherry*)
Maggie Oh, thank you, George. (*To Greta*) You see how useful he's going to be about the house.
Greta What?

Greta and George look at each other, puzzled

Maggie (*to Julie*) I do hope he'll be here soon.
Julie Sorry?
Maggie I'm simply longing to meet him. I'm sure we all are.
Julie Meet who?
Phil (*quickly*) Your father!
Maggie Father? No, I meant…
George Last seen in the bath!
Maggie What?
George Plunging about like a conger eel!
Maggie He can't still be there, surely?

Act II 53

Phil Oh, yes. Very clean these firemen.
Maggie I wasn't meaning her father. We've met him already. (*To Julie*) It was the other one I wanted to meet.
Julie I've only got one father.
Phil Yes. Two fathers would be excessive.
Maggie Surely the poor boy must be back by now?
Julie Back from where?
George (*holding out the drink, abruptly*) Sherry!

Phil dives at Julie and pulls her to her feet just as she is about to accept the drink from George so the sherry is now just out of her reach

Phil You'll have to go and fetch him! You can go out this way. (*He hustles her towards the garden*)
Julie My father?
Phil Tell him we're all waiting! Anxious to meet him!

Phil pushes Julie out into the garden, unceremoniously, and leans breathless on the wall

George reacts to being left with a glass of sherry, shrugs, and drinks it down in one

Maggie I expect he's shy.
Phil Yes. It's that uniform. Very tight fit. Makes him self-conscious when he bends down.
Maggie I wasn't talking about her father!
Greta What's Julie's father doing here anyway?
Maggie He's come to meet her new boyfriend, of course.
Greta (*bemused*) I didn't know she'd *got* a new boyfriend...
Maggie Oh, yes. They've just moved in next door.

This at least makes one thing clear to Greta

Greta Oh, I see! No wonder she didn't mind about you!
Maggie Sorry?
Greta But, Phil—isn't that going to be rather embarrassing for you?
Phil W-what?
Greta Julie living right next door with her latest!
Maggie Why should that embarrass Phil?
Greta Well, wouldn't *you* be embarrassed if your——
Phil (*hastily interrupting*) George! You haven't shown Greta the bathroom!
George I knew there was something. Come on, Greta! I'll show you the bathroom.

Greta I've already been.
Phil Well, now you can go again. Freshen up before dinner.
Greta I'm fresh enough, thank you.
Phil Yes, that's the trouble!
George It's a very nice bathroom.
Greta I never said it wasn't.
George Lovely wallpaper. Beautiful bath.
Phil Yes. With two taps.
Greta Never!
Phil One red and one blue.
Greta The taps?
Phil The tops.
Greta What?
George Tops of the taps. So you know.
Greta Know what?
George Which is which.
Greta What?
George H or C. Oh, come on! (*He pushes Greta towards the hall*)
Maggie Don't let him bully you, Greta. If he speaks to you like that now what will he be like when you're living together?
Greta Living together? (*She looks at George, puzzled*)

Mrs Puffet comes in with some nuts

Puffet Dinner won't be long.
Phil I'm not hungry.
Greta I'm starving.
Puffet Well, I brought you a few more nuts to be going on with. (*She plonks them down on the table*)

Brasset comes in from the garden

Brasset Am I too early?

Mrs Puffet sees him and does not like what she sees at all. She goes to him, urgently

Puffet You can't come in here collecting! This is a private house. Go on—get out of it!
Brasset I beg your pardon?
Puffet I should think so! I've never known such a place for flag days. Can't go down the High Street without being accosted. Go on—hop off! (*She tries to push him out again*)

Act II

Maggie intervenes

Maggie It's all right, Mrs Puffet. He's invited.
Puffet (*appalled*) Invited?
Maggie Yes.
Puffet Here?
Maggie For dinner.
Puffet Oh. Oh, well. Please yourself, I'm sure. (*She glares at Brasset*) Want to watch these lifeboat men, though.

Mrs Puffet stomps off back into the kitchen

Maggie Don't take any notice of her, Percy. She's a little confused.
Greta She's not the only one!
Maggie Let me get you a glass of sherry.
Brasset Thank you.
Greta Have a voddie, dear. Do you the world of good.
Brasset Oh, no. Got to keep my head. There might be an emergency.
George More than likely...!
Brasset Well—where is he?
Phil Sorry?
Brasset I'm anxious to meet him.
Phil Who?
Brasset My future son-in-law. Julie said he was in here.
Maggie Oh, good! He's back, then?
Phil He was. But he went. Popped in and popped out again.
Maggie *I* never saw him. (*She gives the sherry to Brasset*)
Phil No. You were upstairs. He flashed in and flashed out.
George (*helpfully*) In blue.
Phil (*surprised*) What?
George Track suit. All the way down. You remember!
Phil Ah—yes! (*Quietly*) Well done, George!
Brasset What's he doing in a track suit?
Phil Always.
Brasset What?
Phil Jogging. Always jogging. (*He runs on the spot*)
Maggie (*to Brasset*) Don't say he's kept it a secret from you, too? Julie didn't know either.
Brasset Sorry?
Maggie About what he does in private.
George She'll soon find out!
Phil George...!
George Sorry.

Maggie I thought I'd better warn her in case she got a shock if he suddenly started doing it.
Brasset You mean he's doing it *now*?
Phil More than likely.
Brasset But I thought we were going to have dinner?
Maggie We are.
Phil I expect he's working up an appetite. Ah! There he goes! (*He looks out of the window*) Thundering around the flower beds. I'll go and stop him.
Maggie No, Phil. You stay here. George can go.
Phil But I can run faster than George.
George You've had more practice!
Maggie Stay here and entertain everyone.
Phil I don't know any songs.
Maggie (*to George*) If you go out of the front door you'll probably cut him off on the next circuit.
George Yes. Right.

George goes running out into the hall

Brasset Isn't he a bit old for that sort of thing?
Phil Oh, George'll only run very slowly. I hope. Like an old cart-horse.
Brasset No, not George! Julie's ... er...
Phil Oh, him! (*He reacts*) What do you mean a bit old?
Brasset She did warn me.
Phil Did she?
Brasset Oh, yes. Didn't want me to get a nasty surprise.
Maggie Why should meeting your future son-in-law be a nasty surprise?
Brasset Well, you see—he's quite a bit older than she is. In fact, he's nearly as old as I am.
Phil He is not!
Brasset Pardon?
Maggie Phil, there's no need to shout.
Phil Yes, there is! Every reason. He's quite young. Not a day over thirty-seven and completely sound in wind and limb!
Maggie How can you know that? You only met him for a minute.
Phil Possibly. But he made a very big impression.

Julie comes in from the garden

Julie Why is George out there all on his own running round and round the garden?
Brasset He's looking for your——
Phil (*a loud cry of anguish*) Aaah!

They all look at him in astonishment

Ah! I forgot to run the bath out! Come on, Greta. Help me run the bath out! (*He grabs Greta's hand and pulls her towards the hall*)
Greta I'd rather have another voddie.
Phil You can have one upstairs. There's a bottle in the linen cupboard.

Phil drags Greta quickly into the hall and up the stairs

Julie Whatever's the matter with Phil?
Maggie I think he's been eating too many nuts.
Julie Well, Daddy? What do you think of him?
Brasset Who?
Julie My boyfriend.
Brasset If he'd stop running about for five minutes perhaps I could find out!
Julie Well, you can't blame him. I expect he's nervous.
Brasset Well, he's making *me* nervous, too!

Mrs Puffet looks in. She is in some state of alarm

Puffet Bit of a drama in the kitchen, madam!
Maggie What's happened?
Puffet Nothing! That's the trouble. I should be done by now but I'm not cooked properly.

Mrs Puffet goes back into the kitchen

Maggie (*calling after her*) All right, Mrs Puffet. I'll come. (*To Brasset*) Do excuse me.

Maggie goes into the kitchen

Julie I'll come and help you! Now, Daddy—be nice to him.
Brasset If he ever shows up.
Julie What?
Brasset Never mind.

Julie goes into the kitchen

Brasset shakes his head in disbelief at the goings-on

A young man wanders in from the hall. His name is Alan

Alan Er ... excuse me.

Brasset looks at him

This *is* number four?

Brasset rises with a big smile and goes to Alan, enthusiastically

Brasset Well. So you've shown up at last! We thought you were never coming.
Alan (*surprised*) Were you expecting me, then?
Brasset Been expecting you for hours! But I thought you were wearing a track suit...

Alan looks puzzled

Well—how do you do. (*He thrusts out a hand*) I'm her father. (*He shakes Alan's hand, rather vigorously*)
Alan How do you do...
Brasset Hang on a minute. I'll tell them you're here. Be lucky to get any dinner, though. There's a bit of a drama in the kitchen. (*He turns at the kitchen door and looks back*) You know, you're much younger than I thought you'd be.

Brasset goes into the kitchen

George comes running in from the garden, breathless

George It's no good. I can't catch him! (*He sees Alan*) Oh. Sorry. I think I've come into the wrong house...

Puzzled, George runs out again

Alan is even more puzzled

Maggie comes sailing in and moves to Alan, who is facing away from her

Maggie Well, I'm so glad you've stopped running at last.

Alan turns and looks surprised at seeing Maggie. She reacts in horror as she recognizes him

Alan Maggie!
Maggie Alan, darling! What on earth are *you* doing here?

Phil comes in from the hall

It is Maggie's turn to be caught on the hop. Phil looks enquiringly at Alan

Act II

Phil Well—aren't you going to introduce us?

Maggie hesitates, uncertainly

Maggie Haven't you met?
Phil No. I don't think so.
Alan No. Never.
Maggie But you've heard a lot about him!
Phil Have I?
Maggie Yes! Yes, of course you have! (*Clutching at the only possible escape route*) This is—this is Julie's boyfriend!

Phil and Alan both react, but for different reasons

Phil ⎱ (*together*) What?!
Alan ⎰
Phil Are you sure?
Maggie Yes! He's just arrived.
Alan The front door was open.
Phil Blast Mrs Puffet!
Alan Who?
Phil She must have gone out and left everything open.
Alan I think you've got it wrong...
Phil (*belligerently*) Oh, *have* I?
Maggie Of course you have! Mrs Puffet's in the kitchen. Seeing to the dinner. I'd better go back and help her.
Phil No! *I* will.
Maggie Why?
Phil Well, it's my house.
Alan Is it?
Maggie No!
Phil Isn't it?
Maggie So I'll go.
Phil And leave me here with him?
Maggie Oh, dear...! No!
Phil I'd rather go into the kitchen.
Maggie We can't *all* go into the kitchen.
Phil Why not? It's a very large kitchen.
Maggie No. *I*'ll go.
Phil Then I'll go out.
Maggie Oh, good!
Alan Into the garden?
Phil Why not? I've got to stop George before he runs out of puff.

Alan George? (*He is getting more and more bewildered*)
Maggie But that'll leave Alan all alone.
Phil Who the hell's Alan?
Alan I am.
Phil Well, I'm not stopping here with him! He didn't come to see me. I'll tell Julie he's here.
Maggie No!
Phil What?
Maggie Not yet!
Phil But you said he was her boyfriend.
Maggie I know I did.
Phil Then he'd better see her, hadn't he? Presumably that's what he came here for.
Maggie But *I* want to speak to her first! So I'll go into the kitchen and do it.
Phil You mean Julie's in the kitchen as well?
Maggie Yes.
Phil I'm surprised we needed Mrs Puffet.
Alan But Maggie...!
Phil That's *her* name. You knew that?
Alan Yes. We met.
Maggie Just now! He came in through the front door.
Phil I know that!
Alan And there she was.
Maggie So I'll go into the kitchen!
Alan And leave us two together?
Maggie It won't be for long. You may find you have something in common.

Maggie goes into the kitchen

There is an awkward pause as the two men are left alone. Finally, Phil picks up the dish of nuts and offers them ungraciously

Phil Nuts?!
Alan Er ... no, thanks.
Phil (*belligerently*) Don't like them, I suppose?
Alan Well, yes, I like them well enough but...
Phil Just don't care for *my* nuts, is that it?
Alan I didn't mean that...
Phil A drink's more in your line, I suppose?
Alan (*hopefully*) I wouldn't say no.
Phil I thought as much!

But to Alan's disappointment he is not offered one

Act II

Julie comes in from the hall

Julie Hullo, darling!

To Julies surprise, Phil looks far from pleased to see her. He turns to Alan, abruptly

Phil I think she's talking to *you*!
Alan What?
Julie Phil…?
Phil (*rather crossly*) Why aren't you in the kitchen?
Julie I went upstairs.
Phil Maggie hasn't spoken to you, then?
Julie No.
Phil She was very anxious.
Julie Was she?
Phil On her toes like a beagle.
Julie What about?
Phil To tell you about him, I suppose. (*He glares at Alan*)
Julie What about him?
Phil (*crossly*) Well, he's *arrived*, hasn't he?

Julie and Alan look at each other, blankly

Julie Then perhaps you'd introduce us?
Phil It's a bit late for that! I should go and kiss him if I were you.
Julie He may not want me to.
Phil (*to Alan*) You're all right, aren't you?
Alan I was until I came here.
Julie Phil—what's all this about?
Phil Don't ask me! Just kiss him and get it over with!

Maggie comes bustling in from the kitchen and sees Julie

Maggie You weren't in the kitchen!
Phil No. She was upstairs and now she's here and she won't kiss Alan.
Maggie Oh, I think you should!
Julie (*astonished*) What?!
Maggie Well, he's come a very long way.
Julie I'm not here to kiss every weary traveller who walks through your front door.

Maggie laughs emptily and turns to Alan

Maggie She's only joking. Sweet girl. (*Desperately*) Come along, Julie!
Alan (*realizing*) Did you say Julie?
Maggie Yes—precisely!
Alan (*co-operating*) Oh. Well, in that case I suppose I'd better.
Phil Oh, yes—help yourself!
Julie Phil, are you all right?
Phil Don't worry about me! Don't let me stop you. Everyone can kiss who they like. I shall kiss Mrs Puffet in a minute.
Julie What on earth's the matter with you?
Phil You may well ask!
Maggie I expect he's hungry. He'll be all right once we start eating.

George comes running in from the garden

George (*breathlessly*) Well, one thing's certain—he's not out there!
Phil No, he's not. He's in here.
George (*puzzled*) Who?
Phil The one you were looking for.
George Julie's—er...?
Phil Yes!
George You mean you've *told* them?
Phil Didn't have to. Maggie blurted it out.
George Maggie?
Phil (*impatiently*) George—he's in here!
George (*to the others*) Excuse me a minute. (*He takes Phil aside a little*) I know *you* know that, and *I* know that but I didn't think *they* knew that.
Phil Oh, no. They don't. Not that.
George Then what?
Phil Never mind now, George. He's here. Over there! (*He indicates Alan*)

Completely bewildered, George goes to Alan and peers at him, short-sightedly

George Here—wait a bit! Weren't you in that other house I went into just now?
Alan No. It was this one.
George Was it?
Alan (*to Maggie*) You'd better introduce us.

Maggie has no alternative but to continue what she has started

Maggie George, this is Alan. Julie's boyfriend.
Julie (*surprised*) What? I've never even——

Act II

Maggie (*firmly*) Not now, Julie!
Julie Sorry?
Maggie Later.

Julie remains silently bewildered. George is also standing still, stunned

Phil Say something, George.

George turns his head to look, blankly, at Phil

George What?
Phil Say something!
George Now?
Phil Yes.
George Right. (*George turns to Alan again and looks at him for a while without speaking*) Would you care to have a look at the bathroom?
Alan What?
George Lovely wallpaper.
Alan No, thanks.
George Beautiful bath. With two taps. One red and one blue.
Phil (*wearily*) No, George. Not that again!
Alan Look, there's something I...
Maggie (*abruptly*) Why don't you all go for a run in the garden?
Alan What?!
Maggie All you men together. Work up an appetite for dinner.
Alan Am I *staying* for dinner?
Phil Why not? Everybody else is! Look, I'm not going for a run before I find out——
George Might be a good idea.
Phil I want to know what the hell's——
George Phil, what does it matter?
Phil H'm?
George (*pointedly*) I mean, now you're both here—you and Julie's boyfriend—you can all have dinner together, can't you?
Phil Ah! Yes. See what you mean. Safety in numbers. (*With sudden enthusiasm*) Right! Let's have a run, then. Come along, Alan!
Alan Well, I'm not awfully...
Phil Oh, come on!
Alan All right. If I must I must.
Phil Off we go, then!

Phil, George and Alan run out into the garden

Julie turns to Maggie

Julie What was that all about?
Maggie I had to speak to you alone!
Julie Isn't there enough dinner for us all?
Maggie Good heavens—dinner. I'd forgotten all about it. Anyhow, you don't have to worry.
Julie I think I've lost my appetite, anyway. (*She sits on the sofa, despondently*)
Maggie No, not that. Him. You don't have to worry about him.
Julie Who?
Maggie Alan.
Julie I wasn't.

Maggie sits beside her, heavily conspiratorial

Maggie I'll let you into a little secret. He's not *really* your boyfriend.
Julie No. I know he isn't!
Maggie Oh, yes—yes, of course—you would, wouldn't you? Well, the thing is, Julie, I wonder if you'd mind pretending that he *is*. Just for this evening.
Julie Why?
Maggie Well, you see, I couldn't think of anything else to say. He took me by surprise. And it might be a bit embarrassing.
Julie For who?
Maggie For me. If my husband found out.
Julie You mean Alan's come here to see *you*!

Maggie smiles, modestly

Maggie Yes...
Julie Fancy him marching in like that. He must have known your husband would be here.
Maggie He's just like a bulldozer. Won't take no for an answer.
Julie Doesn't George suspect?
Maggie George? Good heavens, George doesn't know anything about it. Anyway, there's nothing to suspect. It's not serious. I mean—nothing actually happened. We met at a party, you see. My husband was away on business and I was there alone, and so was Alan...
Julie And he fancied you?
Maggie (*giggling, self-consciously*) Well, we'd both had a bit to drink and—you know how it is—we got talking and at the end of the evening he said he'd like to see me again.
Julie And did he?
Maggie (*morally*) No, of course not!
Julie Oh.
Maggie But I remember he did say that if I refused to see him again he'd jolly well come and find me.

Act II

Julie And he has!

Maggie So will you do it?

Julie But what about my *real* boyfriend?

Maggie Well, he does seem awfully reluctant to come in out of the garden.

Julie What do you mean? He's been in and out all the evening.

Maggie Well, every time he comes in I seem to be out. Just ask him to keep on running. I'm sure he'll understand. After all—we are going to be neighbours, aren't we?

Brasset comes in from the kitchen, talking as he arrives

Brasset Well, Julie, we found him at last, eh? So now we can all have a nice little chat and—where the hell is he?!

Julie Gone for a run in the garden.

Brasset Again? Doesn't he ever do anything else?

Maggie They all went. Thought they'd work up an appetite for dinner.

Brasset I don't think there's going to *be* any dinner. Mrs Puffet's got her head in the gas oven.

Maggie This is no time for suicide! (*She makes for the kitchen*)

Brasset She's having trouble with her pressure.

Julie I'm not surprised.

Maggie (*turning at the kitchen door and putting on a bright smile*) Dinner parties are such *fun*, aren't they?

Maggie goes into the kitchen

Julie I'd better go and help her. (*She starts to follow*)

Brasset You've come to live next door to some odd people, I can tell you that.

Julie It'll be all right when we've settled down.

Brasset Not much chance of that, is there? Did he *tell* you he was going to spend half his life on the trot?

Julie No—he never mentioned it.

Julie runs out into the kitchen

George runs in from the garden, breathless

George Oh, dear. Oh, dear. It's no good. I'm exhausted. I can't go on any longer...! (*He sinks on to the sofa*)

Brasset Everything all right out there?

George Well, nothing's ablaze, if that's what you mean. But the sky in the west has a tinge of red, and you know what that means.

Mr Brasset's eyes light up

Brasset Fire!!

Brasset rushes hopefully out into the garden

George (*calling after him*) No, no—shepherd's delight! (*He shrugs and sits limply, his head in his hands, getting his breath back*)

Julie comes in from the kitchen

She sees the downcast figure on the sofa and her newly-gained knowledge makes her feel sad for him. She goes and sits beside him, trying to keep back her tears

Julie I ... I can't bear to see you looking like that.

George looks up, vaguely

George What?
Julie Poor George... (*She pats his knee, comfortingly*)
George Sorry?
Julie I promised not to say anything.
George Oh. Oh, I see.
Julie But it upsets me to see you like this.
George Well, it does take a little time at my age. I am over forty, after all. I'll soon be all right.
Julie It's brave of you to say so.

George looks bewildered by this overstatement of his condition

Poor George... (*She pats his knee again*)
George It's not as bad as all that.
Julie I'm glad you think so. That means you'll get over it. Maybe not for a few weeks. Or even a few months. But you will get over it.
George A few *weeks*? I'll be all right in a couple of *minutes*.
Julie I'm glad you think so.
George What are you talking about?
Julie Well ... Alan, of course. (*Sadly*) You know about him, don't you? I can tell.
George I know he's in the garden.
Julie I mean you know what he's been up to...
George I didn't know he'd been up to anything.

Act II

Julie But I thought you were upset.
George No, no. Just a bit out of breath, that's all. Five laps of this house is a long way at my age.
Julie Oh, dear...
George I'll soon be all right. What *has* he been up to?
Julie I'm sorry. I thought you knew.
George Knew what?
Julie Oh, well, I suppose you would have found out sooner or later, anyway.
George Found out what?
Julie It may not be too late. If you act now there's still time to save your marriage.
George I don't know what you're talking about.
Julie I'll have to tell you.
George I wish you would.

Julie takes a deep breath and plunges in

Julie Alan is in love with your wife! They met at a party. He chatted her up and she fell for it. I think they may have been doing it secretly.

A silence. George stares ahead, deep an thought

George Good Lord... Are you sure?"
Julie Positive.
George Rather surprising. My wife doesn't usually go to parties.
Julie Well, now you know why! Because she's vulnerable.
George (*calmly*) Yes. I suppose she must be...
Julie You don't seem very upset.
George Look—how do you know all this?
Julie She told me.
George Did she?
Julie Yes!
George When?
Julie Just now.
George I never heard the telephone go.
Julie What?
George Did you tell her I was having a run in the garden? That would have amused her! (*He laughs*)

Phil comes in from the garden. He sees Julie

Phil Ah! I want a word with you.
Julie (*going to him quickly*) Darling, don't hang about here!

Phil What?

Julie Please do as I say. Just keep on running.

Phil (*puzzled*) Keep on running? I'm exhausted!

Julie I can't explain now, but Maggie doesn't want you here for dinner.

Phil Doesn't she?

Julie No.

Phil Really? Who's going to do the carving?

Julie Well, George will be doing that, naturally!

Phil Oh. Oh, I see. That's all right then. (*To George*) I was worried about the carving, you see. But if you're going to do it, that's all right. You've done it before, I suppose?

Julie So just for this evening—don't hang around!

Phil But I think I'm expected.

Julie Not any more.

Phil Oh. Pity. I'm hungry. Nothing but nuts so far.

George (*helpfully*) There's a Chinese take-away on the corner.

Phil I'd rather stay here...

Julie You don't want to embarrass Maggie, do you?

Phil Er—well, no—I suppose not.

Julie Then do as I say or you will!

Phil Embarrass her?

Julie Certainly.

Phil I see. You can't give me a hint?

Julie No.

Phil I only want to know why——

Julie (*suddenly*) Where have you left my father?

Phil You make him sound like a parcel. He's outside with Alan.

Julie What are they doing?

Phil Looking at the sunset.

Julie You don't suppose they're talking to each other, do you?

Phil Wouldn't be surprised.

Julie (*alarmed*) Oh, no!

Julie rushes out into the garden

Phil What's the matter with her?

George (*deep in thought*) Phil...?

Phil Yes?

George What's all this about Alan being Julie's boyfriend?

Phil Well, that's what Maggie said. And what's more—*he* didn't deny it!

George Good Lord...

Phil I can't understand it, George. (*With due modesty*) After all—Julie said she wanted to marry *me*...

Act II

George Yes.
Phil And it's not like her to have two boyfriends at once. And even if she did, she'd hardly be likely to bring the second one along when the first one was still here.
George Well, *you* did.
Phil That was different! I was *married* to one of them.
George Anyway, I wouldn't give Alan a second thought if I were you.
Phil No?
George (*heavily*) I don't think he's the marrying kind. From what I hear...
Phil Ah! You've heard something about him?
George Yes. As a matter of fact I have.
Phil Well? What is it?

There is a moment's silence

George He's been having it off with Brenda.
Phil What?
George Apparently.
Phil *Your* Brenda?
George Yes.

Phil laughs

Phil Don't be ridiculous! Oh, I don't mean nobody would want to. I simply meant—well, Brenda wouldn't do a thing like that.
George I'm assuming it was he who took the initiative, naturally.
Phil Yes. But she'd be bound to notice. Even Brenda.
George (*thoughtfully*) I can't understand it. Brenda's only interested in horses.
Phil George, I believe we've found a new bond between us. (*He holds out his arms to George*)
George I believe we have. (*He goes into Phil's arms*)
Phil Now we can face him with a united front!

Alan comes running in from the garden

He stops as he is confronted by the sight of Phil and George clasped in each other's arms. He jumps to the wrong conclusion and hesitates, embarrassed

Alan Lovely ... er ... lovely sunset.
Phil (*aggressively*) Are you trying to get into the *Guinness Book of Records*?
Alan Sorry?
George I'm surprised you have the nerve to face us.

Phil We're both trying hard to control ourselves.

Alan is grateful for such small mercies

Alan Oh. Good.

Phil and George come out of their apparent embrace

Phil Didn't you realize that we'd both be here?
Alan Who?
Phil George and I!
Alan I didn't even think about it.
Phil (*appalled*) Good God...!

George faces up to Alan

George Right! Where *was* this party where you met Brenda?

Alan is totally lost

Alan Brenda?
Phil Don't tell me you've forgotten her name already?
Alan I thought her name was Julie.
Phil That was the *other* one.
Alan Two of them?
Phil Certainly. One in the garden. One at home.
Alan But I don't know anyone called Brenda.
George (*exploding*) You met at this party, you chatted her up, and apparently you've been doing it ever since!
Phil And then you come barging in here saying you're Julie's boyfriend as well!
Alan *I* didn't say that! Maggie did!
Phil Anyway, it's quite out of the question because Julie's going to marry *me*.

Alan goes white

Alan Good heavens. You might have killed me.
Phil Yes! That's what we're trying to tell you!
Alan Now, look—before this goes any further—let's get it straight. I don't know anyone called Brenda, and I am not Julie's boyfriend.

Phil and George look at him in silence for a moment

Act II

Phil Then what the hell are you doing here?

Alan gives a little embarrassed laugh

Alan I didn't think you were all going to *be* here. I came here to see ... somebody else.
Phil Somebody else?
Alan Yes.
George Female?
Alan Certainly.
Phil Not Mrs Puffet!
Alan Certainly not!
Phil (*thinking hard*) Not Julie, not Brenda, not Mrs Puffet...
George Shortens the odds a bit.
Phil Not Julie, not Brenda, and not Mrs... (*He realizes and turns to George with a heavy heart*) George, I think we'd better have a drink.
George Right! (*He goes to pour three whiskies*)
Phil (*to Alan*) All right, you may as well tell us and get it over with. Where did you meet her?
Alan Who?
Phil Maggie! Maggie! Where did you meet her?
Alan Oh. At a party.
Phil (*suffering*) I might have guessed...!
Alan I chatted her up a bit. You know how it is.
Phil I'm beginning to find out.

George arrives with the drinks

George Whisky, Alan?
Alan Thanks.
George Whisky, Phil?
Phil Thanks.
George Whisky, George? Thanks. (*He takes a quick sip and moves away to sit down*)

Phil turns to Alan, seething

Phil Well?
Alan Well—er...
Phil Never mind all that! It's getting cold out there, so drink your whisky because you're going to need it.
Alan Am I going out there?
Phil Yes. Head first into the nearest flower bed!

Maggie comes in from the kitchen

Maggie Dinner won't be long.
Phil (*exploding*) Are you cooking it over the pilot light?

Maggie is rather surprised by his manner but ignores it and goes to Alan, playfully

Maggie Alan—she's in the garden.
Alan (*wearily*) What?
Maggie You'd better go and find her, hadn't you?
Phil You needn't bother with all that!
Maggie Sorry?
Phil I know all about it!
Maggie What are you talking about?
Alan I'm sorry, Maggie. I'm afraid I let you down.
Maggie (*alarmed*) You didn't tell them?
Alan Well, you were a bit unfair, you know. I mean, you never said that Phil was going to marry Julie!

Phil reacts in horror at the revelation. George sinks his face into his hand. Maggie turns to look at Phil with a forced smile that could kill

Maggie Darling, what a *lovely* surprise! You never told me that.
Phil Didn't I?
Maggie I'm sure I'd have remembered.
Phil It must have slipped my mind. All these people coming to dinner. I forgot.
Maggie Yes. I bet you did!
Alan He might have killed me.
Phil It's all *his* fault! (*He points an accusing finger at George*) I did ask him to tell you.
Maggie So that's why you were looking so furtive, George?
Phil He's usually so good at that sort of thing.
Maggie Yes, he's never let you down before, has he?
Alan You mean he's *always* going off and getting married?
Maggie Going off, yes. Getting married is a bit of a refinement for him. (*To Phil, sweetly*) So ... you're going to live next door. How cosy.
Phil (*smiling nervously*) Yes, I thought it would be handy. Then you'd know where to find me. If a fuse blows I'll be up the ladder. If the gas goes wonky I'll be here to fix it.
George You see, Maggie, he's not going to stop loving you simply because he's married to somebody else.

Act II

Alan looks confused and goes to Maggie

Alan Excuse me—he's not...?
Maggie Yes.
Alan Married to *you*?
Maggie He was at the last census.
Alan (*to Phil*) But I thought you said——
Phil I did.
Alan But you're already... (*He indicates Maggie*)
Phil I know that.
Alan (*appalled*) You can't go and do that. Not when you've still got one.
Phil Why not?
Alan Because you're already married!
Phil I'm seeing to that.
Maggie Oh? *Are* you? (*She turns to Alan*) Oh, well, that's all right, then, isn't it?
Alan What's all right, then?
Maggie (*secretively*) Well—you know. (*She smiles, saucily*)
Alan (*to Phil*) But a moment ago you were being all possessive about *her*! (*He indicates Maggie*)
Maggie Were you? Oh, darling, how sweet.
Alan You can't go around being possessive about a wife you're trying to get rid of!
George (*helpfully*) Oh, I dunno. If you want to sell a car you don't stop driving it the moment the ad goes in the newspaper.

They all look at George in astonishment

Alan That's about the most disgusting remark I've ever heard!
Phil Yes, George. You've gone too far.
George I was only trying to ... explain the situation.
Phil Well, you have, George. You have. Very clearly.
Maggie When will you be moving in next door, darling? You must remember to send me a change of address card. Oh, and one thing I must know. Where did you meet her? On a number forty-seven?
George Forty-nine.
Maggie Yes, of course. How silly of me. Forty-nine. Same as last time. How romantic.
Phil (*suddenly*) Just a minute! What am *I* feeling guilty about? How about *you*?
Maggie What?
Phil Where *was* this party?
Maggie (*vaguely*) Party?

Phil When you "happened" to bump into Alan, and he chatted you up and all that. I've heard all about it, you know.
Maggie Oh? Really? (*to Alan*) You *have* been busy, haven't you?
Phil You—you don't admit it, do you?
Maggie Certainly.
Alan \
Phil / (*together*) What?!
Alan You mean you aren't going to deny it?
Maggie Not much point, is there? He was bound to find out sooner or later. (*To Phil*) You're not angry, are you?
Phil Well, I was *going* to be.
Maggie But, darling, it is my turn.
Alan Look, I think I ought to explain...
Maggie (*abruptly*) Will you please keep out of this?
Alan Oh. Sorry. (*He withdraws*)
Phil You'll go on living here, I suppose?
Maggie Oh, yes. I'm not contemplating marriage.
Alan (*alarmed*) Marriage?
Maggie Not yet, anyhow.
Phil Just a good time.
Maggie Certainly.
Alan (*intervening*) Look, there's something I——
Phil I'm talking to my wife!
Alan Oh. Sorry. (*He withdraws again*)
Maggie You do want me to stay on here, presumably? Then if you're next door at least you'll know where I am. If your flowers need arranging I'll be here to fix them. If your shirts need ironing I'll be here to do them too.

George sniggers. Phil glares at him and he covers up. Alan hastens to make his escape

Alan Will you excuse me a minute? I think I left my engine running.
Maggie Dinner won't be long, darling. (*She gives him a light kiss*)
Alan Oh. Right. Yes.

Alan goes quickly out into the hall

George is deep in thought

Maggie I'm so glad you like him.
Phil I didn't say I liked him!
Maggie We met at a party...
Phil (*crossly*) I know!

Maggie There's no need to be snappy just because you always meet yours in the open air.

George (*gazing into space thoughtfully*) I still can't understand why Brenda should ring up to tell a perfect stranger that she'd been having it off with a man she'd never met... (*Puzzled, he tries to work it out, mouthing soundlessly to himself*)

Phil and Maggie watch him for a moment

Maggie What's he talking about?
Phil I dunno. He often talks like that when he's hungry.

Julie comes in from the garden

Julie It's all right. Daddy's watching television.
Phil In the garden?
Julie In the house next door. (*She advances on Phil*) I told you not to hang about!
Phil I'm just going!
Julie I'm sorry, Maggie.
Maggie Oh, that's all right. My husband knows all about me and Alan.
Julie Yes. I know. (*She looks sadly at George*) Poor George...
Maggie (*icily*) And *I* know all about *you*!
Julie Well, of course you do. That was never a secret.
Maggie Really? He just forget to tell *me* about it? Well, I hope you and my husband will be very happy! (*She turns away*)

Phil hastily grabs George and pushes him towards Julie

Phil Yes, we all hope that!

Loyal to the last, George attempts to carry it off

George I'm sure we will be! (*He trots across and enfolds Julie in his arms*)

Julie looks astonished and pushes him away with an affectionate laugh

Julie George, don't be silly! Go on, then.
George What?
Julie (*indicating Maggie*) Grab her while you've still got the chance! (*She urges George towards Maggie*)

He makes a last desperate attempt to stop the cat getting out of the bag. He trots across to Maggie, holding his arms out, and embraces her like a bear. Maggie, naturally, looks astonished. Phil waits for the inevitable. Maggie extricates herself, pushing George gently aside on to the sofa, and goes with a determined tread to Julie

Maggie I think there's something you should know.
Phil I don't think she wants to know that! Do you, Julie? No, you don't! No, she doesn't!
Maggie Oh, yes, she does! (*To Julie*) George and I are not married.

Julie looks at Phil

Julie Is that true?
Phil Yes, that's true. George and I are not married.
Julie (*to Maggie*) That doesn't matter. Not nowadays. Weddings aren't important. It's being together that counts.
Maggie Julie dear, do try to understand. I am married. But I'm not married to George.
Julie Is your husband still alive?
Maggie And kicking! I'll give you a hint. He is—*in—this—room*.
George Game, set and match...

Julie looks at Phil, suddenly furious

Julie *You!*
Phil (*nervously*) Ah—yes—well——
Julie No wonder you didn't want to come here for dinner!

Julie storms out into the garden

Phil starts to tollow

Phil Julie, I...! (*But she has gone*) I really must stop travelling on buses.

Phil goes out after Julie

Maggie Oh, dear. Was I a bit hard on him?
George (*with a smile*) Well, it was your turn.
Maggie You're very fond of Phil, aren't you?
George I've known him a long time.
Maggie So I suppose you'd do *anything* to help him. Even pretend to be married to me.
George Oh, that wasn't very difficult.

Act II

Maggie looks at him with surprise and delight

Maggie George!
George (*sheepishly*) Well, I mean—I'm fond of you, too. As a matter of fact, when I first met you, I... (*He stops and looks away, fearful of going too far*) Oh, dear...!

Maggie sits beside him, smiling delightedly

Maggie Go on, George! Don't stop *now*!
George Well—when I first met you, I ... I quite fancied you, as a matter of fact.
Maggie Not any more?
George Well, I—I mean—it's different now, isn't it?
Maggie And I never knew...
George (*anxiously*) Look—you won't tell Phil about this, will you? I mean—not a word—not *ever*.
Maggie I promise. It'll be our little secret. (*She kisses him on the cheek*)

Mrs Puffet comes in from the kitchen and sees George being kissed

He leaps away from Maggie, guiltily. Mrs Puffet eyes them, suspiciously

Puffet There's a funny popping noise in your oven!
Maggie (*serenely*) I don't mind the noise so long as it's cooking the food.
Puffet You'd better come and see for yourself. I don't like the sound of it. Not one bit I don't.
Maggie Then I'll come now, Mrs Puffet.
Puffet Not dragging you away, am I?

Mrs Puffet gives George a baleful look and goes back into the kitchen

Maggie (*smiling at George*) Now I've ruined your reputation!

Maggie runs out into the kitchen

Brasset comes in from the hall, pushing Alan ahead of him

Brasset I want to know what you've done to her!
Alan I haven't done anything!
Brasset Then why has she packed?
Alan I didn't even know she'd *un*packed.
Brasset (*to George*) He was running again.

George Round the garden?
Brasset Down the road. I spotted him from the window and cut him off before he reached his car.
George You weren't trying to get away, were you, Alan?

Alan looks sheepish

Brasset You'll have to do better than this when you're married, you know.
Alan I'm not going to be!
Brasset What?
Alan Not if I can help it.
Brasset But you told Julie…!
Alan That wasn't me! That was the other one!

There is an explosion and a clatter of saucepans from inside the kitchen. They all react in alarm

Brasset What on earth was that?

Maggie races in from the kitchen amidst a cloud of smoke and carrying a charred tea towel

Maggie Ah! Mr Brasset! Just the man we want!
Brasset What's happened?
Maggie There's a small conflagration in the kitchen.
Brasset (*his eyes brightening*) Fire?
Maggie Well, there are flames!
Brasset That's what I like to hear!

Brasset rushes off into the kitchen, delightedly, with Maggie following in his wake

George has had enough and heads for the garden

Alan Where are *you* going?
George I thought I'd have a quick run before dinner.

George trots out into the garden

Greta comes in from the hall, cradling a badly depleted bottle of vodka in her arms like a baby. She is walking a trifle unsteadily and wearing a happy smile

Alan Greta! So there you are!

Act II   79

Greta tries to focus in his direction

Greta Who's that?
Alan It's me! I thought perhaps you weren't here after all.
Greta I've been sitting in the linen cupboard drinking vodka. (*She giggles and comes to rest on the sofa*)
Alan I almost drove off and left you.

Greta peers at him, hazily

Greta Do I know you?
Alan Don't say you've forgotten?
Greta What?
Alan It's *me*!
Greta Who?
Alan Alan! We met at a party and made a date!
Greta Did we? (*She peers at him more closely and smiles as a light dawns dimly*) Oh, yes. I think I *do* remember you! Vaguely…
Alan I went to your place to pick you up but you weren't there.
Greta No. I was here! How did you know where to find me?
Alan Your flatmate gave me this address.
Greta So how long have you been here?
Alan About an hour. And they're all mad!

Maggie comes out of the kitchen in businesslike fashion and crosses briskly round below the sofa to get the soda-syphon from the drinks cupboard, talking as she goes

Maggie Hullo, Greta. So glad you're still here. We've been neglecting you dreadfully, I'm afraid. I do hope you've been helping yourself to the vodka. Oh, yes—I see you have! We're having a little trouble in the kitchen and now he wants this. Are you looking for George? He's probably gone back into the garden. They're all so dreadfully athletic, aren't they? (*To Alan*) I won't be long, darling.

Maggie kisses Alan briefly on the forehead as she passes and goes smoothly back into the kitchen with the soda-syphon

Greta Why was that lady kissing you?
Alan Because *she* thinks I came here looking for *her*.
Greta Why?
Alan Well—I go to a *lot* of parties.

Phil comes in from the garden. He sees Greta

Phil Good heavens! I'd forgotten all about you!
Greta I've been sitting in the linen cupboard...
Phil Oh, good! (*He glances around*) Any sign of dinner? Not a lot, no. Pity. I'm famished. I take it you two have met? Been introduced and all that? I know we're in the middle of a crisis but don't let's forget our manners.
Alan We didn't *need* to be introduced. We'd already met.
Phil Where?
Alan At a party.
Phil You seem to spend your whole life in the midst of a social whirl.
Greta But *I* didn't invite him *here*!
Phil I know you didn't. (*He glares at Alan*) He came here to see Maggie!
Greta Oh, well, that's another one off your hands, then. (*To Alan*) He's been a bit oversubscribed this evening. Three girls in one house.
Alan Three? How do you manage it?
Phil London Transport! Well, go on—you'll find Maggie in the kitchen.
Alan But I didn't come here for Maggie!
Phil You... You didn't?
Alan No.
Phil But I thought you said...?
Alan No. That was what *she* said.
Phil Oh, I *see*...
Alan Sorry.
Phil (*with a big smile*) Oh, don't be sorry. I'm delighted!
Alan Are you?
Phil So you never met her at a party?
Alan Oh, yes. We met at a party all right.
Phil But you didn't say what she *thinks* you said?
Alan (*a little shamefaced*) I may have said it. Probably meant it at the time, too.

Phil is beginning to relish the situation

Phil But you didn't actually come here to see Maggie?
Alan I'd no idea she lived here! It was quite a surprise I can tell you when she suddenly wandered in from the kitchen.
Phil So what *did* you come here for?
Alan I came for *her*. (*He indicates Greta*)
Phil (*delightedly*) Oh—then you'd better get her out of here, hadn't you? (*He urges them both towards the hall*)
Greta You needn't be in quite such a hurry to get rid of me.
Phil (*gleefully*) Well, I'm longing to have a little chat with my wife!
Greta Don't say that *she*'s here, as well?
Phil What? (*Suddenly*) Do I smell burning?

Act II

Alan (*casually*) Probably. The kitchen's on fire.
Phil What?!
Alan It's all right, though. The fireman chap's seeing to it.
Phil Seeing to it? It smells as if he's stoking it!

Phil rushes out into the kitchen

Alan I don't think we're going to get any dinner.
Greta No. Even the nuts are all finished.
Alan Well—my car's just around the corner.
Greta Oh, good!

Julie and George come in from the garden. She is ready to leave. He is carrying some of her things

George (*as they come in*) You're sure you won't change your mind?
Julie I can't stay here. Not now.
Alan Well—can *I* give you a lift, then?
Greta Alan!
Alan Both of us, that is!
Julie Thank you very much.
George Are you all leaving, then?
Alan Yes. It's been *lovely*, but we think we ought to go.
Greta Besides, we're hungry.

Brasset comes in from the kitchen, beaming with joy

Brasset Nicest little kitchen fire I've seen for a long time. That soda syphon really did the trick. Should be part of standard equipment.
Julie (*to Alan*) Have you got room for my father?
Alan (*without enthusiasm*) Yes, I suppose so. (*He starts to go*)
Greta Alan...?
Alan What?
Greta Have you got any vodka in *your* linen cupboard?

Alan and Greta go out into the hall

Julie Come on, then, Daddy. (*She pushes him towards the hall*)
Brasset But I haven't had my dinner yet...
Julie You'll get it later.

She pushes Brasset, protesting, after the others

She turns back to George. He gives the cases to her

You will explain to Phil, won't you?
George (*smiling, warmly*) I usually do.

Julie gives him a quick kiss and goes out into the hall after the others

Phil and Maggie come in from the kitchen

Phil Talk about a sledge-hammer to crack a walnut! You'd have thought he was attacking the Great Fire of London out there.
Maggie (*to George*) Where are the others?
George They've gone.
Phil All of them?
George Yes.
Phil Good heavens...
Maggie What an extraordinary way to behave.
Phil Doesn't look as if we'll be getting any dinner tonight. Everything's black out there.
George Well, there's that Chinese take-away on the corner. I'll go and get something, shall I?
Phil Good idea! And I'll open some wine.

Mrs Puffet comes in from the kitchen. She has her hat on, ready to leave, and her face is streaked with black

Puffet Well, that's it! I've had enough and I'm off! What's my husband going to say when he sees my face?
George He must be used to it by now.
Puffet That's enough of that! You'd better run me home on account of what you did to my little banger.
George Oh, no! I've done enough running for one night!

George escapes hastily into the hall

Puffet Sorry about the dinner, madam.
Maggie It wasn't your fault. It's just been one of those days, hasn't it?
Puffet It certainly has! Started with a bump up me backside and ended with a bang in me oven!

Mrs Puffet goes off into the hall

Maggie and Phil are left alone. He goes to pour a drink

Phil Drink?

Act II   83

Maggie Yes. I think I could do with one.
Phil Whisky?
Maggie Anything. As long as it's a large one.

Phil pours two whiskies, brings them to her and they sit side-by-side on the sofa. Maggie smiles, miscievously

I suppose we'll have to give this back to Julie.
Phil (*carefully*) H'm? Sorry?
Maggie The sofa, darling.
Phil Ah. Yes.
Maggie George can help you carry it.
Phil Yes. Cheers.
Maggie Cheers.

They drink. A pause. Then Phil chuckles, gleefully

What's the matter with *you*?
Phil (*airily*) Nothing. Nothing... (*He pats her knee with overdone sympathy*) Never mind...
Maggie What do you mean "never mind"?
Phil (*amused*) You and your feller...
Maggie (*innocently*) I don't know what you're talking about.
Phil All that stuff about you and Alan. He didn't really come here looking for you, did he?
Maggie Apparently not, as he seems to have gone.
Phil Never mind... (*He pats her knee again with heavily elaborate sympathy*) You didn't really expect me to believe all that, did you?
Maggie (*coolly*) I suppose not. (*A beat*) You were bound to find out the truth sooner or later.
Phil You bet! (*He sips his drink, happily*)
Maggie I could hardly expect you to believe *that* story for long.
Phil Not a chance! (*He chuckles, contentedly*)
Maggie Still, it was worth a try. At least it stopped you suspecting anything else.
Phil Yes... (*He looks at her*) Sorry?
Maggie (*vaguely*) Nothing.
Phil What did you say?
Maggie I said it was worth a try.
Phil No. After that.
Maggie I said it stopped you suspecting anything else.
Phil And what does that mean?
Maggie Darling, don't ask so many questions. Hadn't you better open that wine? The food'll be here in a minute.

Phil I want to know what you're talking about!
Maggie (*enigmatically*) Well, darling ... you are out quite a lot, after all. It does get a bit boring all on your own.
Phil You mean there *is* someone else? Is that it? Is that what you're trying to tell me?
Maggie I'm not trying to tell you anything. But you will keep asking questions.
Phil I see. (*He pauses sullenly*) You wouldn't care to tell me who he is?
Maggie Yes.
Phil (*surprised*) You would?
Maggie If you really want to know. But it'll be a bit embarrassing...
Phil Who is it?
Maggie Do you promise you won't make a scene? I don't want you stamping up and down and spoiling the evening.
Phil Who is it?
Maggie Can't you guess?
Phil No, I can't! Who the hell is it?
Maggie Well... George, of course!

Phil gazes at her

Phil George?
Maggie Yes.
Phil *My* George?
Maggie No—*my* George!

A moment, then Phil starts to laugh

Phil I don't believe it! George?
Maggie Believe what you like. It happens to be true.
Phil No—never! Not George. When?
Maggie Whenever we had the opportunity. Whenever you weren't at home.
Phil You mean whenever I popped out, he popped in?
Maggie Yes.

Phil is torn between belief and disbelief. He laughs again

Phil No, no! I'm sorry. It's impossible. He'd never do a thing like that. Not with *my* wife.
Maggie Why not? *You* weren't doing it with your wife.
Phil No. Not that. Not George. I'll ask him!
Maggie He'll deny it, of course.
Phil Because it isn't true!

Act II

Maggie Because he's a gentleman.
Phil Because it never happened!
Maggie Didn't you ever wonder why I always believed the alibis George made up for you?
Phil Well, yes I... What?
Maggie It made it so easy for *us*.
Phil (*shattered*) Good God...!
Maggie (*getting her own back*) Never mind...! (*She pats his knee with elaborate masculine sympathy*)

Phil simmers for a moment, then he persuades himself that she is making it up and starts to laugh, albeit a little forced

Phil Oh, darling, I do love you!
Maggie Is that quite tactful, under the circumstances?
Phil Fancy thinking up a story like that! Just to get me back.
Maggie (*unimpressed*) Is that what I've got?
Phil Isn't that what you wanted?
Maggie (*coolly*) I hadn't really thought about it. (*She gets up*)
Phil Where are you going?
Maggie To get some more nuts. (*She heads for the kitchen*)
Phil I can't get over it. You making up a story like that! (*He chuckles*)

Maggie stops at the kitchen door

Maggie Phil—don't keep on about it. You don't have to believe it if you don't want to.
Phil (*laughing*) No, I don't want to! And I won't, what's more!
Maggie (*blithely*) All right. All right. (*Then she puts the knife in*) You'll never be *certain*, though, will you?

Maggie sails out to the kitchen

Phil sits still, unable to believe and yet not completely able to discard the possibility

George walks in from the hall with a plastic bag containing Chinese food in containers

George (*brightly*) Here we are! I wasn't very long, was I? (*He goes to put down the Chinese food on the table near the armchair*)

Phil looks at George with new eyes, wondering, suspecting... George becomes aware of his look

Everything all right?
Phil I'm not sure.
George Oh. (*He continues unpacking the food*)
Phil George…?
George H'm?
Phil There's something I'd like to talk to you about.
George (*unconcerned*) Oh, yes?
Phil It's about you and Maggie.

George reacts with alarm

George Good Lord, she didn't *tell* you, did she?

Phil starts to rise, looking at George in astonishment, thinking the worst as——

—*the* CURTAIN *falls*

FURNITURE AND PROPERTY LIST

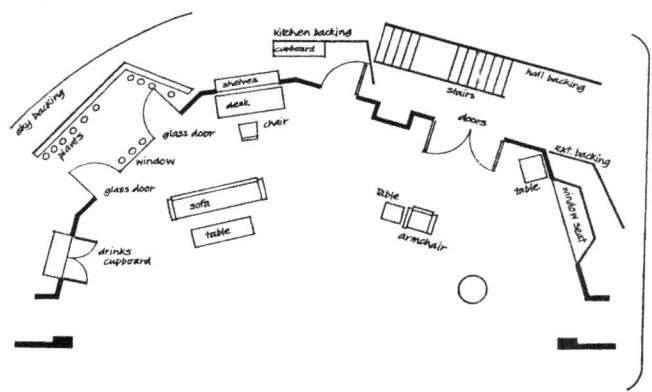

ACT I

Scene 1

On stage: Sofa. *On it*: 3 cushions
Coffee table. *On it*: fruit bowl
Armchair
Small armchair table. *On it*: ornament
Pouffe
Drinks cupboard. *On it*: bottle of whisky, bottle of vodka, bottle of sherry, soda syphon, 4 whisky glasses, 4 vodka glasses, 4 sherry glasses. *On shelf above*: ice-bucket with ice, 3 small bowls, 1 tin of cheese biscuits, 1 packet of twiglets, 1 tin of salted peanuts
Artist's desk. *On it*: lamp, artist's brushes in jar, magazines, sketch pad, various canvases
Desk chair
Table. *On it*: lamp, telephone, telephone directories under
Waste-paper basket
Window seat. *On it*: 2 cushions, various magazines

On walls: various paintings, sketches, Express Dairy calendar (*over desk*)
On shelves: various books and ornaments
Carpet

Off stage: Fleamarket hessian bag, 2 plastic carrier bags, small suitcase, brown shoulder bag; all full (**Julie**)
Large canvas shoulder bag. *In it*: packing, artist's brushes fastened with elastic band, roll of white cartridge paper, bag of oranges (**Maggie**)
2 canvases in holder (**Maggie**)
1 carrier bag of shopping, 2 bottles of red wine in tissue paper (**Maggie**)

Personal: **George:** wristwatch
Maggie: handbag. *In it*: purse, car keys
Brasset: wallet

Scene 2

Off stage: 2 folding tubular garden chairs (**Maggie**)
Bowl of salted peanuts (**Mrs Puffet**)
Apron (**Maggie**)

Personal: **Greta:** handbag
Maggie: apron

ACT II

Off stage: 2 bowls of salted peanuts (**Mrs Puffet**)
Slightly charred tea towel (**Maggie**)
Almost empty bottle of vodka (**Greta**)
Black pancake make-up, tissues, mirror, bowl of water (**Mrs Puffet**)
Julie's things (**George**)
White plastic carrier bag. *In it*: 5 silver-foil containers of Chinese food (**George**)

LIGHTING PLOT

Property fittings required: desk lamp, table lamp, concealed lighting over drinks cupboard or wall brackets
1 interior. The same throughout

ACT I, SCENE 1. Afternoon

To open: Bright, warm summer light with sunshine flooding in from the garden

Cue 1   **Phil** and **George** embrace   (Page 28)
           Black-out

ACT I, SCENE 2. Evening

To open: Warm summer sunshine: outside, hint of pink in the sky. Still bright in room. All interior lights on

Cue 2   **George** looks alarmed   (Page 44)
           Black-out

ACT II   As close of previous act

No cues

EFFECTS PLOT

ACT I

Cue 1   Black-out   (Page 28)
Music until start of Scene 2

ACT II

Cue 2   **Alan**: "That was the other one!"   (Page 78)
Explosion and clatter of falling saucepans in kitchen

Cue 3   **Maggie** comes in from kitchen   (Page 78)
Drifting smoke from kitchen

www.ingramcontent.com/pod-product-compliance
Ingram Content Group UK Ltd.
Pitfield, Milton Keynes, MK11 3LW, UK
UKHW021840210426
5322IPUK00022B/380